C-2397 CAREER EXAMINATION SERIES

This is your
PASSBOOK for...

Transit Property Protection Agent

Test Preparation Study Guide
Questions & Answers

COPYRIGHT NOTICE

This book is SOLELY intended for, is sold ONLY to, and its use is RESTRICTED to individual, bona fide applicants or candidates who qualify by virtue of having seriously filed applications for appropriate license, certificate, professional and/or promotional advancement, higher school matriculation, scholarship, or other legitimate requirements of education and/or governmental authorities.

This book is NOT intended for use, class instruction, tutoring, training, duplication, copying, reprinting, excerption, or adaptation, etc., by:

1) Other publishers
2) Proprietors and/or Instructors of "Coaching" and/or Preparatory Courses
3) Personnel and/or Training Divisions of commercial, industrial, and governmental organizations
4) Schools, colleges, or universities and/or their departments and staffs, including teachers and other personnel
5) Testing Agencies or Bureaus
6) Study groups which seek by the purchase of a single volume to copy and/or duplicate and/or adapt this material for use by the group as a whole without having purchased individual volumes for each of the members of the group
7) Et al.

Such persons would be in violation of appropriate Federal and State statutes.

PROVISION OF LICENSING AGREEMENTS – Recognized educational, commercial, industrial, and governmental institutions and organizations, and others legitimately engaged in educational pursuits, including training, testing, and measurement activities, may address request for a licensing agreement to the copyright owners, who will determine whether, and under what conditions, including fees and charges, the materials in this book may be used them. In other words, a licensing facility exists for the legitimate use of the material in this book on other than an individual basis. However, it is asseverated and affirmed here that the material in this book CANNOT be used without the receipt of the express permission of such a licensing agreement from the Publishers. Inquiries re licensing should be addressed to the company, attention rights and permissions department.

All rights reserved, including the right of reproduction in whole or in part, in any form or by any means, electronic or mechanical, including photocopying, recording, or by any information storage and retrieval system, without permission in writing from the Publisher.

Copyright © 2024 by
National Learning Corporation

212 Michael Drive, Syosset, NY 11791
(516) 921-8888 • www.passbooks.com
E-mail: info@passbooks.com

PUBLISHED IN THE UNITED STATES OF AMERICA

PASSBOOK® SERIES

THE *PASSBOOK® SERIES* has been created to prepare applicants and candidates for the ultimate academic battlefield – the examination room.

At some time in our lives, each and every one of us may be required to take an examination – for validation, matriculation, admission, qualification, registration, certification, or licensure.

Based on the assumption that every applicant or candidate has met the basic formal educational standards, has taken the required number of courses, and read the necessary texts, the *PASSBOOK® SERIES* furnishes the one special preparation which may assure passing with confidence, instead of failing with insecurity. Examination questions – together with answers – are furnished as the basic vehicle for study so that the mysteries of the examination and its compounding difficulties may be eliminated or diminished by a sure method.

This book is meant to help you pass your examination provided that you qualify and are serious in your objective.

The entire field is reviewed through the huge store of content information which is succinctly presented through a provocative and challenging approach – the question-and-answer method.

A climate of success is established by furnishing the correct answers at the end of each test.

You soon learn to recognize types of questions, forms of questions, and patterns of questioning. You may even begin to anticipate expected outcomes.

You perceive that many questions are repeated or adapted so that you can gain acute insights, which may enable you to score many sure points.

You learn how to confront new questions, or types of questions, and to attack them confidently and work out the correct answers.

You note objectives and emphases, and recognize pitfalls and dangers, so that you may make positive educational adjustments.

Moreover, you are kept fully informed in relation to new concepts, methods, practices, and directions in the field.

You discover that you are actually taking the examination all the time: you are preparing for the examination by "taking" an examination, not by reading extraneous and/or supererogatory textbooks.

In short, this PASSBOOK®, used directedly, should be an important factor in helping you to pass your test.

TRANSIT PROPERTY PROTECTION AGENT

DUTIES
Transit Property Protection Agents perform routine work in the surveillance of subway stations, train yards and adjacent grounds on Transit Authority property in order to provide protection against terrorist acts, trespass, damage and loss; make written reports; read, interpret, and follow special written instructions and directives; drive a motor vehicle; and perform related work.

EXAMPLES OF TYPICAL TASKS
Some of the physical activities performed by Transit Property Protection Agents and environmental conditions experienced are: standing for lengthy periods of time, including standing at posts and patrolling facilities; staying continuously alert; walking up and down stairs and over extended distances that cover the perimeter of Transit properties; hearing alarms from doors, cars, etc.; confronting unauthorized persons on Transit Authority properties; walking along subway tracks where a live third rail is present; and working outside in all kinds of weather.

SCOPE OF THE EXAM
The written test will be of the multiple-choice type and may include questions which will test for: reading, understanding and following directives, rules, regulations and written instructions; taking proper actions in emergency situations; filling out required forms, writing reports and keeping records; understanding and following safety and first aid procedures; understanding military time; job-related arithmetic; and other related areas.

HOW TO TAKE A TEST

I. YOU MUST PASS AN EXAMINATION

A. *WHAT EVERY CANDIDATE SHOULD KNOW*

Examination applicants often ask us for help in preparing for the written test. What can I study in advance? What kinds of questions will be asked? How will the test be given? How will the papers be graded?

As an applicant for a civil service examination, you may be wondering about some of these things. Our purpose here is to suggest effective methods of advance study and to describe civil service examinations.

Your chances for success on this examination can be increased if you know how to prepare. Those "pre-examination jitters" can be reduced if you know what to expect. You can even experience an adventure in good citizenship if you know why civil service exams are given.

B. *WHY ARE CIVIL SERVICE EXAMINATIONS GIVEN?*

Civil service examinations are important to you in two ways. As a citizen, you want public jobs filled by employees who know how to do their work. As a job seeker, you want a fair chance to compete for that job on an equal footing with other candidates. The best-known means of accomplishing this two-fold goal is the competitive examination.

Exams are widely publicized throughout the nation. They may be administered for jobs in federal, state, city, municipal, town or village governments or agencies.

Any citizen may apply, with some limitations, such as the age or residence of applicants. Your experience and education may be reviewed to see whether you meet the requirements for the particular examination. When these requirements exist, they are reasonable and applied consistently to all applicants. Thus, a competitive examination may cause you some uneasiness now, but it is your privilege and safeguard.

C. *HOW ARE CIVIL SERVICE EXAMS DEVELOPED?*

Examinations are carefully written by trained technicians who are specialists in the field known as "psychological measurement," in consultation with recognized authorities in the field of work that the test will cover. These experts recommend the subject matter areas or skills to be tested; only those knowledges or skills important to your success on the job are included. The most reliable books and source materials available are used as references. Together, the experts and technicians judge the difficulty level of the questions.

Test technicians know how to phrase questions so that the problem is clearly stated. Their ethics do not permit "trick" or "catch" questions. Questions may have been tried out on sample groups, or subjected to statistical analysis, to determine their usefulness.

Written tests are often used in combination with performance tests, ratings of training and experience, and oral interviews. All of these measures combine to form the best-known means of finding the right person for the right job.

II. HOW TO PASS THE WRITTEN TEST

A. NATURE OF THE EXAMINATION

To prepare intelligently for civil service examinations, you should know how they differ from school examinations you have taken. In school you were assigned certain definite pages to read or subjects to cover. The examination questions were quite detailed and usually emphasized memory. Civil service exams, on the other hand, try to discover your present ability to perform the duties of a position, plus your potentiality to learn these duties. In other words, a civil service exam attempts to predict how successful you will be. Questions cover such a broad area that they cannot be as minute and detailed as school exam questions.

In the public service similar kinds of work, or positions, are grouped together in one "class." This process is known as *position-classification*. All the positions in a class are paid according to the salary range for that class. One class title covers all of these positions, and they are all tested by the same examination.

B. FOUR BASIC STEPS

1) Study the announcement

How, then, can you know what subjects to study? Our best answer is: "Learn as much as possible about the class of positions for which you've applied." The exam will test the knowledge, skills and abilities needed to do the work.

Your most valuable source of information about the position you want is the official exam announcement. This announcement lists the training and experience qualifications. Check these standards and apply only if you come reasonably close to meeting them.

The brief description of the position in the examination announcement offers some clues to the subjects which will be tested. Think about the job itself. Review the duties in your mind. Can you perform them, or are there some in which you are rusty? Fill in the blank spots in your preparation.

Many jurisdictions preview the written test in the exam announcement by including a section called "Knowledge and Abilities Required," "Scope of the Examination," or some similar heading. Here you will find out specifically what fields will be tested.

2) Review your own background

Once you learn in general what the position is all about, and what you need to know to do the work, ask yourself which subjects you already know fairly well and which need improvement. You may wonder whether to concentrate on improving your strong areas or on building some background in your fields of weakness. When the announcement has specified "some knowledge" or "considerable knowledge," or has used adjectives like "beginning principles of..." or "advanced ... methods," you can get a clue as to the number and difficulty of questions to be asked in any given field. More questions, and hence broader coverage, would be included for those subjects which are more important in the work. Now weigh your strengths and weaknesses against the job requirements and prepare accordingly.

3) Determine the level of the position

Another way to tell how intensively you should prepare is to understand the level of the job for which you are applying. Is it the entering level? In other words, is this the position in which beginners in a field of work are hired? Or is it an intermediate or advanced level? Sometimes this is indicated by such words as "Junior" or "Senior" in the class title. Other jurisdictions use Roman numerals to designate the level – Clerk I, Clerk II, for example. The word "Supervisor" sometimes appears in the title. If the level is not indicated by the title, check the description of duties. Will you be working under very close supervision, or will you have responsibility for independent decisions in this work?

4) Choose appropriate study materials

Now that you know the subjects to be examined and the relative amount of each subject to be covered, you can choose suitable study materials. For beginning level jobs, or even advanced ones, if you have a pronounced weakness in some aspect of your training, read a modern, standard textbook in that field. Be sure it is up to date and has general coverage. Such books are normally available at your library, and the librarian will be glad to help you locate one. For entry-level positions, questions of appropriate difficulty are chosen – neither highly advanced questions, nor those too simple. Such questions require careful thought but not advanced training.

If the position for which you are applying is technical or advanced, you will read more advanced, specialized material. If you are already familiar with the basic principles of your field, elementary textbooks would waste your time. Concentrate on advanced textbooks and technical periodicals. Think through the concepts and review difficult problems in your field.

These are all general sources. You can get more ideas on your own initiative, following these leads. For example, training manuals and publications of the government agency which employs workers in your field can be useful, particularly for technical and professional positions. A letter or visit to the government department involved may result in more specific study suggestions, and certainly will provide you with a more definite idea of the exact nature of the position you are seeking.

III. KINDS OF TESTS

Tests are used for purposes other than measuring knowledge and ability to perform specified duties. For some positions, it is equally important to test ability to make adjustments to new situations or to profit from training. In others, basic mental abilities not dependent on information are essential. Questions which test these things may not appear as pertinent to the duties of the position as those which test for knowledge and information. Yet they are often highly important parts of a fair examination. For very general questions, it is almost impossible to help you direct your study efforts. What we can do is to point out some of the more common of these general abilities needed in public service positions and describe some typical questions.

1) General information

Broad, general information has been found useful for predicting job success in some kinds of work. This is tested in a variety of ways, from vocabulary lists to questions about current events. Basic background in some field of work, such as sociology or economics, may be sampled in a group of questions. Often these are principles which have become familiar to most persons through exposure rather than through formal training. It is difficult to advise you how to study for these questions; being alert to the world around you is our best suggestion.

2) Verbal ability

An example of an ability needed in many positions is verbal or language ability. Verbal ability is, in brief, the ability to use and understand words. Vocabulary and grammar tests are typical measures of this ability. Reading comprehension or paragraph interpretation questions are common in many kinds of civil service tests. You are given a paragraph of written material and asked to find its central meaning.

3) Numerical ability

Number skills can be tested by the familiar arithmetic problem, by checking paired lists of numbers to see which are alike and which are different, or by interpreting charts and graphs. In the latter test, a graph may be printed in the test booklet which you are asked to use as the basis for answering questions.

4) Observation

A popular test for law-enforcement positions is the observation test. A picture is shown to you for several minutes, then taken away. Questions about the picture test your ability to observe both details and larger elements.

5) Following directions

In many positions in the public service, the employee must be able to carry out written instructions dependably and accurately. You may be given a chart with several columns, each column listing a variety of information. The questions require you to carry out directions involving the information given in the chart.

6) Skills and aptitudes

Performance tests effectively measure some manual skills and aptitudes. When the skill is one in which you are trained, such as typing or shorthand, you can practice. These tests are often very much like those given in business school or high school courses. For many of the other skills and aptitudes, however, no short-time preparation can be made. Skills and abilities natural to you or that you have developed throughout your lifetime are being tested.

Many of the general questions just described provide all the data needed to answer the questions and ask you to use your reasoning ability to find the answers. Your best preparation for these tests, as well as for tests of facts and ideas, is to be at your physical and mental best. You, no doubt, have your own methods of getting into an exam-taking mood and keeping "in shape." The next section lists some ideas on this subject.

IV. KINDS OF QUESTIONS

Only rarely is the "essay" question, which you answer in narrative form, used in civil service tests. Civil service tests are usually of the short-answer type. Full instructions for answering these questions will be given to you at the examination. But in case this is your first experience with short-answer questions and separate answer sheets, here is what you need to know:

1) Multiple-choice Questions

Most popular of the short-answer questions is the "multiple choice" or "best answer" question. It can be used, for example, to test for factual knowledge, ability to solve problems or judgment in meeting situations found at work.

A multiple-choice question is normally one of three types—
- It can begin with an incomplete statement followed by several possible endings. You are to find the one ending which *best* completes the statement, although some of the others may not be entirely wrong.
- It can also be a complete statement in the form of a question which is answered by choosing one of the statements listed.

- It can be in the form of a problem – again you select the best answer.

Here is an example of a multiple-choice question with a discussion which should give you some clues as to the method for choosing the right answer:

When an employee has a complaint about his assignment, the action which will *best* help him overcome his difficulty is to
- A. discuss his difficulty with his coworkers
- B. take the problem to the head of the organization
- C. take the problem to the person who gave him the assignment
- D. say nothing to anyone about his complaint

In answering this question, you should study each of the choices to find which is best. Consider choice "A" – Certainly an employee may discuss his complaint with fellow employees, but no change or improvement can result, and the complaint remains unresolved. Choice "B" is a poor choice since the head of the organization probably does not know what assignment you have been given, and taking your problem to him is known as "going over the head" of the supervisor. The supervisor, or person who made the assignment, is the person who can clarify it or correct any injustice. Choice "C" is, therefore, correct. To say nothing, as in choice "D," is unwise. Supervisors have and interest in knowing the problems employees are facing, and the employee is seeking a solution to his problem.

2) True/False Questions

The "true/false" or "right/wrong" form of question is sometimes used. Here a complete statement is given. Your job is to decide whether the statement is right or wrong.

SAMPLE: A roaming cell-phone call to a nearby city costs less than a non-roaming call to a distant city.

This statement is wrong, or false, since roaming calls are more expensive.

This is not a complete list of all possible question forms, although most of the others are variations of these common types. You will always get complete directions for answering questions. Be sure you understand *how* to mark your answers – ask questions until you do.

V. RECORDING YOUR ANSWERS

Computer terminals are used more and more today for many different kinds of exams.

For an examination with very few applicants, you may be told to record your answers in the test booklet itself. Separate answer sheets are much more common. If this separate answer sheet is to be scored by machine – and this is often the case – it is highly important that you mark your answers correctly in order to get credit.

An electronic scoring machine is often used in civil service offices because of the speed with which papers can be scored. Machine-scored answer sheets must be marked with a pencil, which will be given to you. This pencil has a high graphite content which responds to the electronic scoring machine. As a matter of fact, stray dots may register as answers, so do not let your pencil rest on the answer sheet while you are pondering the correct answer. Also, if your pencil lead breaks or is otherwise defective, ask for another.

Since the answer sheet will be dropped in a slot in the scoring machine, be careful not to bend the corners or get the paper crumpled.

The answer sheet normally has five vertical columns of numbers, with 30 numbers to a column. These numbers correspond to the question numbers in your test booklet. After each number, going across the page are four or five pairs of dotted lines. These short dotted lines have small letters or numbers above them. The first two pairs may also have a "T" or "F" above the letters. This indicates that the first two pairs only are to be used if the questions are of the true-false type. If the questions are multiple choice, disregard the "T" and "F" and pay attention only to the small letters or numbers.

Answer your questions in the manner of the sample that follows:

32. The largest city in the United States is
    A. Washington, D.C.
    B. New York City
    C. Chicago
    D. Detroit
    E. San Francisco

1) Choose the answer you think is best. (New York City is the largest, so "B" is correct.)
2) Find the row of dotted lines numbered the same as the question you are answering. (Find row number 32)
3) Find the pair of dotted lines corresponding to the answer. (Find the pair of lines under the mark "B.")
4) Make a solid black mark between the dotted lines.

VI. BEFORE THE TEST

Common sense will help you find procedures to follow to get ready for an examination. Too many of us, however, overlook these sensible measures. Indeed, nervousness and fatigue have been found to be the most serious reasons why applicants fail to do their best on civil service tests. Here is a list of reminders:

- Begin your preparation early – Don't wait until the last minute to go scurrying around for books and materials or to find out what the position is all about.
- Prepare continuously – An hour a night for a week is better than an all-night cram session. This has been definitely established. What is more, a night a week for a month will return better dividends than crowding your study into a shorter period of time.
- Locate the place of the exam – You have been sent a notice telling you when and where to report for the examination. If the location is in a different town or otherwise unfamiliar to you, it would be well to inquire the best route and learn something about the building.
- Relax the night before the test – Allow your mind to rest. Do not study at all that night. Plan some mild recreation or diversion; then go to bed early and get a good night's sleep.
- Get up early enough to make a leisurely trip to the place for the test – This way unforeseen events, traffic snarls, unfamiliar buildings, etc. will not upset you.
- Dress comfortably – A written test is not a fashion show. You will be known by number and not by name, so wear something comfortable.

- Leave excess paraphernalia at home – Shopping bags and odd bundles will get in your way. You need bring only the items mentioned in the official notice you received; usually everything you need is provided. Do not bring reference books to the exam. They will only confuse those last minutes and be taken away from you when in the test room.
- Arrive somewhat ahead of time – If because of transportation schedules you must get there very early, bring a newspaper or magazine to take your mind off yourself while waiting.
- Locate the examination room – When you have found the proper room, you will be directed to the seat or part of the room where you will sit. Sometimes you are given a sheet of instructions to read while you are waiting. Do not fill out any forms until you are told to do so; just read them and be prepared.
- Relax and prepare to listen to the instructions
- If you have any physical problem that may keep you from doing your best, be sure to tell the test administrator. If you are sick or in poor health, you really cannot do your best on the exam. You can come back and take the test some other time.

VII. AT THE TEST

The day of the test is here and you have the test booklet in your hand. The temptation to get going is very strong. Caution! There is more to success than knowing the right answers. You must know how to identify your papers and understand variations in the type of short-answer question used in this particular examination. Follow these suggestions for maximum results from your efforts:

1) Cooperate with the monitor

The test administrator has a duty to create a situation in which you can be as much at ease as possible. He will give instructions, tell you when to begin, check to see that you are marking your answer sheet correctly, and so on. He is not there to guard you, although he will see that your competitors do not take unfair advantage. He wants to help you do your best.

2) Listen to all instructions

Don't jump the gun! Wait until you understand all directions. In most civil service tests you get more time than you need to answer the questions. So don't be in a hurry. Read each word of instructions until you clearly understand the meaning. Study the examples, listen to all announcements and follow directions. Ask questions if you do not understand what to do.

3) Identify your papers

Civil service exams are usually identified by number only. You will be assigned a number; you must not put your name on your test papers. Be sure to copy your number correctly. Since more than one exam may be given, copy your exact examination title.

4) Plan your time

Unless you are told that a test is a "speed" or "rate of work" test, speed itself is usually not important. Time enough to answer all the questions will be provided, but this does not mean that you have all day. An overall time limit has been set. Divide the total time (in minutes) by the number of questions to determine the approximate time you have for each question.

5) Do not linger over difficult questions

If you come across a difficult question, mark it with a paper clip (useful to have along) and come back to it when you have been through the booklet. One caution if you do this – be sure to skip a number on your answer sheet as well. Check often to be sure that you have not lost your place and that you are marking in the row numbered the same as the question you are answering.

6) Read the questions

Be sure you know what the question asks! Many capable people are unsuccessful because they failed to *read* the questions correctly.

7) Answer all questions

Unless you have been instructed that a penalty will be deducted for incorrect answers, it is better to guess than to omit a question.

8) Speed tests

It is often better NOT to guess on speed tests. It has been found that on timed tests people are tempted to spend the last few seconds before time is called in marking answers at random – without even reading them – in the hope of picking up a few extra points. To discourage this practice, the instructions may warn you that your score will be "corrected" for guessing. That is, a penalty will be applied. The incorrect answers will be deducted from the correct ones, or some other penalty formula will be used.

9) Review your answers

If you finish before time is called, go back to the questions you guessed or omitted to give them further thought. Review other answers if you have time.

10) Return your test materials

If you are ready to leave before others have finished or time is called, take ALL your materials to the monitor and leave quietly. Never take any test material with you. The monitor can discover whose papers are not complete, and taking a test booklet may be grounds for disqualification.

VIII. EXAMINATION TECHNIQUES

1) Read the general instructions carefully. These are usually printed on the first page of the exam booklet. As a rule, these instructions refer to the timing of the examination; the fact that you should not start work until the signal and must stop work at a signal, etc. If there are any *special* instructions, such as a choice of questions to be answered, make sure that you note this instruction carefully.

2) When you are ready to start work on the examination, that is as soon as the signal has been given, read the instructions to each question booklet, underline any key words or phrases, such as *least, best, outline, describe* and the like. In this way you will tend to answer as requested rather than discover on reviewing your paper that you *listed without describing*, that you selected the *worst* choice rather than the *best* choice, etc.

3) If the examination is of the objective or multiple-choice type – that is, each question will also give a series of possible answers: A, B, C or D, and you are called upon to select the best answer and write the letter next to that answer on your answer paper – it is advisable to start answering each question in turn. There may be anywhere from 50 to 100 such questions in the three or four hours allotted and you can see how much time would be taken if you read through all the questions before beginning to answer any. Furthermore, if you come across a question or group of questions which you know would be difficult to answer, it would undoubtedly affect your handling of all the other questions.

4) If the examination is of the essay type and contains but a few questions, it is a moot point as to whether you should read all the questions before starting to answer any one. Of course, if you are given a choice – say five out of seven and the like – then it is essential to read all the questions so you can eliminate the two that are most difficult. If, however, you are asked to answer all the questions, there may be danger in trying to answer the easiest one first because you may find that you will spend too much time on it. The best technique is to answer the first question, then proceed to the second, etc.

5) Time your answers. Before the exam begins, write down the time it started, then add the time allowed for the examination and write down the time it must be completed, then divide the time available somewhat as follows:
   - If 3-1/2 hours are allowed, that would be 210 minutes. If you have 80 objective-type questions, that would be an average of 2-1/2 minutes per question. Allow yourself no more than 2 minutes per question, or a total of 160 minutes, which will permit about 50 minutes to review.
   - If for the time allotment of 210 minutes there are 7 essay questions to answer, that would average about 30 minutes a question. Give yourself only 25 minutes per question so that you have about 35 minutes to review.

6) The most important instruction is to *read each question* and make sure you know what is wanted. The second most important instruction is to *time yourself properly* so that you answer every question. The third most important instruction is to *answer every question*. Guess if you have to but include something for each question. Remember that you will receive no credit for a blank and will probably receive some credit if you write something in answer to an essay question. If you guess a letter – say "B" for a multiple-choice question – you may have guessed right. If you leave a blank as an answer to a multiple-choice question, the examiners may respect your feelings but it will not add a point to your score. Some exams may penalize you for wrong answers, so in such cases *only*, you may not want to guess unless you have some basis for your answer.

7) Suggestions
   a. Objective-type questions
      1. Examine the question booklet for proper sequence of pages and questions
      2. Read all instructions carefully
      3. Skip any question which seems too difficult; return to it after all other questions have been answered
      4. Apportion your time properly; do not spend too much time on any single question or group of questions

5. Note and underline key words – *all, most, fewest, least, best, worst, same, opposite*, etc.
6. Pay particular attention to negatives
7. Note unusual option, e.g., unduly long, short, complex, different or similar in content to the body of the question
8. Observe the use of "hedging" words – *probably, may, most likely*, etc.
9. Make sure that your answer is put next to the same number as the question
10. Do not second-guess unless you have good reason to believe the second answer is definitely more correct
11. Cross out original answer if you decide another answer is more accurate; do not erase until you are ready to hand your paper in
12. Answer all questions; guess unless instructed otherwise
13. Leave time for review

b. Essay questions
1. Read each question carefully
2. Determine exactly what is wanted. Underline key words or phrases.
3. Decide on outline or paragraph answer
4. Include many different points and elements unless asked to develop any one or two points or elements
5. Show impartiality by giving pros and cons unless directed to select one side only
6. Make and write down any assumptions you find necessary to answer the questions
7. Watch your English, grammar, punctuation and choice of words
8. Time your answers; don't crowd material

8) Answering the essay question

Most essay questions can be answered by framing the specific response around several key words or ideas. Here are a few such key words or ideas:

M's: manpower, materials, methods, money, management
P's: purpose, program, policy, plan, procedure, practice, problems, pitfalls, personnel, public relations

a. Six basic steps in handling problems:
1. Preliminary plan and background development
2. Collect information, data and facts
3. Analyze and interpret information, data and facts
4. Analyze and develop solutions as well as make recommendations
5. Prepare report and sell recommendations
6. Install recommendations and follow up effectiveness

b. Pitfalls to avoid
1. *Taking things for granted* – A statement of the situation does not necessarily imply that each of the elements is necessarily true; for example, a complaint may be invalid and biased so that all that can be taken for granted is that a complaint has been registered

2. *Considering only one side of a situation* – Wherever possible, indicate several alternatives and then point out the reasons you selected the best one
3. *Failing to indicate follow up* – Whenever your answer indicates action on your part, make certain that you will take proper follow-up action to see how successful your recommendations, procedures or actions turn out to be
4. *Taking too long in answering any single question* – Remember to time your answers properly

IX. AFTER THE TEST

Scoring procedures differ in detail among civil service jurisdictions although the general principles are the same. Whether the papers are hand-scored or graded by machine we have described, they are nearly always graded by number. That is, the person who marks the paper knows only the number – never the name – of the applicant. Not until all the papers have been graded will they be matched with names. If other tests, such as training and experience or oral interview ratings have been given, scores will be combined. Different parts of the examination usually have different weights. For example, the written test might count 60 percent of the final grade, and a rating of training and experience 40 percent. In many jurisdictions, veterans will have a certain number of points added to their grades.

After the final grade has been determined, the names are placed in grade order and an eligible list is established. There are various methods for resolving ties between those who get the same final grade – probably the most common is to place first the name of the person whose application was received first. Job offers are made from the eligible list in the order the names appear on it. You will be notified of your grade and your rank as soon as all these computations have been made. This will be done as rapidly as possible.

People who are found to meet the requirements in the announcement are called "eligibles." Their names are put on a list of eligible candidates. An eligible's chances of getting a job depend on how high he stands on this list and how fast agencies are filling jobs from the list.

When a job is to be filled from a list of eligibles, the agency asks for the names of people on the list of eligibles for that job. When the civil service commission receives this request, it sends to the agency the names of the three people highest on this list. Or, if the job to be filled has specialized requirements, the office sends the agency the names of the top three persons who meet these requirements from the general list.

The appointing officer makes a choice from among the three people whose names were sent to him. If the selected person accepts the appointment, the names of the others are put back on the list to be considered for future openings.

That is the rule in hiring from all kinds of eligible lists, whether they are for typist, carpenter, chemist, or something else. For every vacancy, the appointing officer has his choice of any one of the top three eligibles on the list. This explains why the person whose name is on top of the list sometimes does not get an appointment when some of the persons lower on the list do. If the appointing officer chooses the second or third eligible, the No. 1 eligible does not get a job at once, but stays on the list until he is appointed or the list is terminated.

X. HOW TO PASS THE INTERVIEW TEST

The examination for which you applied requires an oral interview test. You have already taken the written test and you are now being called for the interview test – the final part of the formal examination.

You may think that it is not possible to prepare for an interview test and that there are no procedures to follow during an interview. Our purpose is to point out some things you can do in advance that will help you and some good rules to follow and pitfalls to avoid while you are being interviewed.

What is an interview supposed to test?

The written examination is designed to test the technical knowledge and competence of the candidate; the oral is designed to evaluate intangible qualities, not readily measured otherwise, and to establish a list showing the relative fitness of each candidate – as measured against his competitors – for the position sought. Scoring is not on the basis of "right" and "wrong," but on a sliding scale of values ranging from "not passable" to "outstanding." As a matter of fact, it is possible to achieve a relatively low score without a single "incorrect" answer because of evident weakness in the qualities being measured.

Occasionally, an examination may consist entirely of an oral test – either an individual or a group oral. In such cases, information is sought concerning the technical knowledges and abilities of the candidate, since there has been no written examination for this purpose. More commonly, however, an oral test is used to supplement a written examination.

Who conducts interviews?

The composition of oral boards varies among different jurisdictions. In nearly all, a representative of the personnel department serves as chairman. One of the members of the board may be a representative of the department in which the candidate would work. In some cases, "outside experts" are used, and, frequently, a businessman or some other representative of the general public is asked to serve. Labor and management or other special groups may be represented. The aim is to secure the services of experts in the appropriate field.

However the board is composed, it is a good idea (and not at all improper or unethical) to ascertain in advance of the interview who the members are and what groups they represent. When you are introduced to them, you will have some idea of their backgrounds and interests, and at least you will not stutter and stammer over their names.

What should be done before the interview?

While knowledge about the board members is useful and takes some of the surprise element out of the interview, there is other preparation which is more substantive. It *is* possible to prepare for an oral interview – in several ways:

1) Keep a copy of your application and review it carefully before the interview

This may be the only document before the oral board, and the starting point of the interview. Know what education and experience you have listed there, and the sequence and dates of all of it. Sometimes the board will ask you to review the highlights of your experience for them; you should not have to hem and haw doing it.

2) Study the class specification and the examination announcement

Usually, the oral board has one or both of these to guide them. The qualities, characteristics or knowledges required by the position sought are stated in these documents. They offer valuable clues as to the nature of the oral interview. For example, if the job involves supervisory responsibilities, the announcement will usually indicate that knowledge of modern supervisory methods and the qualifications of the candidate as a supervisor will be tested. If so, you can expect such questions, frequently in the form of a hypothetical situation which you are expected to solve. NEVER go into an oral without knowledge of the duties and responsibilities of the job you seek.

3) Think through each qualification required

Try to visualize the kind of questions you would ask if you were a board member. How well could you answer them? Try especially to appraise your own knowledge and background in each area, *measured against the job sought*, and identify any areas in which you are weak. Be critical and realistic – do not flatter yourself.

4) Do some general reading in areas in which you feel you may be weak

For example, if the job involves supervision and your past experience has NOT, some general reading in supervisory methods and practices, particularly in the field of human relations, might be useful. Do NOT study agency procedures or detailed manuals. The oral board will be testing your understanding and capacity, not your memory.

5) Get a good night's sleep and watch your general health and mental attitude

You will want a clear head at the interview. Take care of a cold or any other minor ailment, and of course, no hangovers.

What should be done on the day of the interview?

Now comes the day of the interview itself. Give yourself plenty of time to get there. Plan to arrive somewhat ahead of the scheduled time, particularly if your appointment is in the fore part of the day. If a previous candidate fails to appear, the board might be ready for you a bit early. By early afternoon an oral board is almost invariably behind schedule if there are many candidates, and you may have to wait. Take along a book or magazine to read, or your application to review, but leave any extraneous material in the waiting room when you go in for your interview. In any event, relax and compose yourself.

The matter of dress is important. The board is forming impressions about you – from your experience, your manners, your attitude, and your appearance. Give your personal appearance careful attention. Dress your best, but not your flashiest. Choose conservative, appropriate clothing, and be sure it is immaculate. This is a business interview, and your appearance should indicate that you regard it as such. Besides, being well groomed and properly dressed will help boost your confidence.

Sooner or later, someone will call your name and escort you into the interview room. *This is it.* From here on you are on your own. It is too late for any more preparation. But remember, you asked for this opportunity to prove your fitness, and you are here because your request was granted.

What happens when you go in?

The usual sequence of events will be as follows: The clerk (who is often the board stenographer) will introduce you to the chairman of the oral board, who will introduce you to the other members of the board. Acknowledge the introductions before you sit down. Do not be surprised if you find a microphone facing you or a stenotypist sitting by. Oral interviews are usually recorded in the event of an appeal or other review.

Usually the chairman of the board will open the interview by reviewing the highlights of your education and work experience from your application – primarily for the benefit of the other members of the board, as well as to get the material into the record. Do not interrupt or comment unless there is an error or significant misinterpretation; if that is the case, do not hesitate. But do not quibble about insignificant matters. Also, he will usually ask you some question about your education, experience or your present job – partly to get you to start talking and to establish the interviewing "rapport." He may start the actual questioning, or turn it over to one of the other members. Frequently, each member undertakes the questioning on a particular area, one in which he is perhaps most competent, so you can expect each member to participate in the examination. Because time is limited, you may also expect some rather abrupt switches in the direction the questioning takes, so do not be upset by it. Normally, a board member will not pursue a single line of questioning unless he discovers a particular strength or weakness.

After each member has participated, the chairman will usually ask whether any member has any further questions, then will ask you if you have anything you wish to add. Unless you are expecting this question, it may floor you. Worse, it may start you off on an extended, extemporaneous speech. The board is not usually seeking more information. The question is principally to offer you a last opportunity to present further qualifications or to indicate that you have nothing to add. So, if you feel that a significant qualification or characteristic has been overlooked, it is proper to point it out in a sentence or so. Do not compliment the board on the thoroughness of their examination – they have been sketchy, and you know it. If you wish, merely say, "No thank you, I have nothing further to add." This is a point where you can "talk yourself out" of a good impression or fail to present an important bit of information. Remember, *you close the interview yourself.*

The chairman will then say, "That is all, Mr. _____, thank you." Do not be startled; the interview is over, and quicker than you think. Thank him, gather your belongings and take your leave. Save your sigh of relief for the other side of the door.

How to put your best foot forward

Throughout this entire process, you may feel that the board individually and collectively is trying to pierce your defenses, seek out your hidden weaknesses and embarrass and confuse you. Actually, this is not true. They are obliged to make an appraisal of your qualifications for the job you are seeking, and they want to see you in your best light. Remember, they must interview all candidates and a non-cooperative candidate may become a failure in spite of their best efforts to bring out his qualifications. Here are 15 suggestions that will help you:

1) Be natural – Keep your attitude confident, not cocky

If you are not confident that you can do the job, do not expect the board to be. Do not apologize for your weaknesses, try to bring out your strong points. The board is interested in a positive, not negative, presentation. Cockiness will antagonize any board member and make him wonder if you are covering up a weakness by a false show of strength.

2) Get comfortable, but don't lounge or sprawl

Sit erectly but not stiffly. A careless posture may lead the board to conclude that you are careless in other things, or at least that you are not impressed by the importance of the occasion. Either conclusion is natural, even if incorrect. Do not fuss with your clothing, a pencil or an ashtray. Your hands may occasionally be useful to emphasize a point; do not let them become a point of distraction.

3) Do not wisecrack or make small talk

This is a serious situation, and your attitude should show that you consider it as such. Further, the time of the board is limited – they do not want to waste it, and neither should you.

4) Do not exaggerate your experience or abilities

In the first place, from information in the application or other interviews and sources, the board may know more about you than you think. Secondly, you probably will not get away with it. An experienced board is rather adept at spotting such a situation, so do not take the chance.

5) If you know a board member, do not make a point of it, yet do not hide it

Certainly you are not fooling him, and probably not the other members of the board. Do not try to take advantage of your acquaintanceship – it will probably do you little good.

6) Do not dominate the interview

Let the board do that. They will give you the clues – do not assume that you have to do all the talking. Realize that the board has a number of questions to ask you, and do not try to take up all the interview time by showing off your extensive knowledge of the answer to the first one.

7) Be attentive

You only have 20 minutes or so, and you should keep your attention at its sharpest throughout. When a member is addressing a problem or question to you, give him your undivided attention. Address your reply principally to him, but do not exclude the other board members.

8) Do not interrupt

A board member may be stating a problem for you to analyze. He will ask you a question when the time comes. Let him state the problem, and wait for the question.

9) Make sure you understand the question

Do not try to answer until you are sure what the question is. If it is not clear, restate it in your own words or ask the board member to clarify it for you. However, do not haggle about minor elements.

10) Reply promptly but not hastily

A common entry on oral board rating sheets is "candidate responded readily," or "candidate hesitated in replies." Respond as promptly and quickly as you can, but do not jump to a hasty, ill-considered answer.

11) Do not be peremptory in your answers

A brief answer is proper – but do not fire your answer back. That is a losing game from your point of view. The board member can probably ask questions much faster than you can answer them.

12) Do not try to create the answer you think the board member wants

He is interested in what kind of mind you have and how it works – not in playing games. Furthermore, he can usually spot this practice and will actually grade you down on it.

13) Do not switch sides in your reply merely to agree with a board member

Frequently, a member will take a contrary position merely to draw you out and to see if you are willing and able to defend your point of view. Do not start a debate, yet do not surrender a good position. If a position is worth taking, it is worth defending.

14) Do not be afraid to admit an error in judgment if you are shown to be wrong

The board knows that you are forced to reply without any opportunity for careful consideration. Your answer may be demonstrably wrong. If so, admit it and get on with the interview.

15) Do not dwell at length on your present job

The opening question may relate to your present assignment. Answer the question but do not go into an extended discussion. You are being examined for a *new* job, not your present one. As a matter of fact, try to phrase ALL your answers in terms of the job for which you are being examined.

Basis of Rating

Probably you will forget most of these "do's" and "don'ts" when you walk into the oral interview room. Even remembering them all will not ensure you a passing grade. Perhaps you did not have the qualifications in the first place. But remembering them will help you to put your best foot forward, without treading on the toes of the board members.

Rumor and popular opinion to the contrary notwithstanding, an oral board wants you to make the best appearance possible. They know you are under pressure – but they also want to see how you respond to it as a guide to what your reaction would be under the pressures of the job you seek. They will be influenced by the degree of poise you display, the personal traits you show and the manner in which you respond.

ABOUT THIS BOOK

This book contains tests divided into Examination Sections. Go through each test, answering every question in the margin. We have also attached a sample answer sheet at the back of the book that can be removed and used. At the end of each test look at the answer key and check your answers. On the ones you got wrong, look at the right answer choice and learn. Do not fill in the answers first. Do not memorize the questions and answers, but understand the answer and principles involved. On your test, the questions will likely be different from the samples. Questions are changed and new ones added. If you understand these past questions you should have success with any changes that arise. Tests may consist of several types of questions. We have additional books on each subject should more study be advisable or necessary for you. Finally, the more you study, the better prepared you will be. This book is intended to be the last thing you study before you walk into the examination room. Prior study of relevant texts is also recommended. NLC publishes some of these in our Fundamental Series. Knowledge and good sense are important factors in passing your exam. Good luck also helps. So now study this Passbook, absorb the material contained within and take that knowledge into the examination. Then do your best to pass that exam.

EXAMINATION SECTION

EXAMINATION SECTION
TEST 1

DIRECTIONS: Each question or incomplete statement is followed by several suggested answers or completions. Select the one that BEST answers the question or completes the statement. *PRINT THE LETTER OF THE CORRECT ANSWER IN THE SPACE AT THE RIGHT.*

1. Which one of the following persons who has been injured in an accident should be the FIRST to be given first aid?
    A

    A. woman with a surface cut on her leg
    B. man with a sprained wrist
    C. man with a deep cut on the cheek which is bleeding profusely
    D. woman who complains that her left hand feels broken

2. *Protection Agents are not allowed to read newspapers while on duty.*
   Which of the following is the MAIN reason for this rule?

    A. They may be distracted from their duties.
    B. They are not being paid to read newspapers.
    C. Such reading may lull them to sleep.
    D. Newspaper ink may come off on their hands.

3. The operator of a Transit Authority van hands Protection Agent Johnson a Material Pass listing the following: 31 boxes of No. 10 letter envelopes, 11 boxes - each containing 24 bottles of correction fluid, 18 packages of 14-inch photocopy paper, 12 packages of 11-inch photocopy paper, and 10 packages of paper towels. Agent Johnson counts the boxes and packages and finds a total of 79.
   How many boxes or packages are missing?

   A. 2   B. 3   C. 4   D. 5

4. *It is a violation of rules for a Protection Agent to carry a firearm while on Transit Authority property. The possession of such a weapon, whether carried on the person, in a personal vehicle, or stored in a locker, can result in charges being filed against the Agent.*
   According to the above information, the carrying of a firearm

    A. on Authority property by any employee is prohibited
    B. anywhere by an Agent is prohibited under all circumstances
    C. on Authority property by an Agent is prohibited under all circumstances
    D. anywhere by an Authority employee may be reason for charges being filed against that employee

5. *News reporters may enter Authority property if they have the written authorisation of a Public Affairs Department official. The Agent on duty must get permission from the Property Protection Control Desk before admitting to the property a news person who has no such written authorisation.*
   If a reporter tells a Protection Agent that she has received permission from the Authority President to enter the property, what is the FIRST thing the Agent should do?

A. Call the Authority police.
B. Admit the reporter immediately.
C. Call the Authority President's office.
D. Call the Property Protection Control Desk.

Questions 6-10.

DIRECTIONS: Questions 6 through 10 are to be answered SOLELY on the basis of the information in the paragraphs below titled FIRES AND EXTINGUISHERS.

FIRES AND EXTINGUISHERS

There are four classes of fires.

Trash fires, paper fires, cloth fires, wood fires, etc. are classified as Class A fires. Water or a water-base solution should be used to extinguish Class A fires. They also can be extinguished by covering the combustibles with a multi-purpose dry chemical.

Burning liquids, gasoline, oil, paint, tar, etc. are considered Class B fires. Such fires can be extinguished by smothering or blanketing them. Extinguishers used for Class B fires are Halon, CO_2, or multi-purpose dry chemical. Water tends to spread such fires and should not be used.

Fires in electrical equipment and switchboards are classified as Class C fires. When live electrical equipment is involved, a non-conducting extinguishing agent like CO_2, a multi-purpose dry chemical, or Halon should always be used. Soda-acid or other water-type extinguishers should not be used.

Class D fires consist of burning metals in finely-divided forms like chips, turnings, and shavings. Specially-designed extinguishing agents that provide a smothering blanket or coating should be used to extinguish Class D fires. Multi-purpose dry-powder extinguishants are such agents.

6. The ONLY type of extinguishing agent that can be used on any type of fire is

    A. a multi-purpose, dry-chemical, extinguishing agent
    B. soda-acid
    C. water
    D. carbon dioxide

7. A fire in litter swept from a subway car in a yard is MOST likely to be a Class _____ fire.

    A. A   B. B   C. C   D. D

8. Fire coming from the underbody of a subway car is MOST likely to be a Class _____ fire.

    A. A   B. B   C. C   D. D

9. Which of the following extinguishing agents should NOT be used in fighting a Class C fire involving live electrical equipment?

    A. Halon
    B. CO_2

C. A multi-purpose dry chemical
D. Soda-acid

10. Water is NOT recommended for use on Class B fires because water   10.____

    A. would cool the fire
    B. evaporates too quickly
    C. might spread the fire
    D. would smother the fire

11. *An Officer on duty at a bus depot is required to have visitors sign a Visitor's Release form before admitting them to the property.*   11.____
    William Johnson, a tool manufacturer's representative, appears at the Ulmer Park bus depot to keep an appointment with Supervisor Walter Minton. Harold Martin, the Officer on duty, phones Mr. Minton, who tells him that he may admit Mr. Johnson. Mr. Johnson, however, refuses to sign a Visitor's Release form.
    Which of the following should Officer Martin do FIRST?

    A. Call the Property Protection Control Desk.
    B. Courteously explain to Mr. Johnson that rules require visitors to sign such forms before they can be admitted.
    C. Call Mr. Minton to tell him that Mr. Johnson refused to sign the release and that he cannot admit him.
    D. Call the Transit Police.

Questions 12-18.

DIRECTIONS: Questions 12 through 18 are to be answered SOLELY on the basis of the information given in the paragraph below and the Visitor's Release form.

On Friday, December 19, at 9:15 A.M., Joan Sanford, who represented the Adam Hart Manufacturing Company, appeared at the Property Protection Agent booth at the 207th Street, Manhattan, Main Shop. She stated that she wanted to see Superintendent Patterson about a parts contract with her firm, which makes spare parts for subway cars. The Agent called Mr. Patterson, who said he expected her. The Agent thereupon asked her to complete a Visitor's Release form, which she did. On the form, she indicated her age as 27, her occupation as salesperson, her supervisor's name as Lawrence Austin, the firm's location at 1427 Cedar St., Glendale, N.Y., and her home address as 25-16 65th Road, Oak Point, N.Y. Agent Paul Jones signed the Visitor's Release form as witness to her signature. She then entered the facility and left Transit Authority property at 2 P.M., at which time Mr. Jones gave Miss Sanford a copy of the Visitor's Release form.

Transit Authority   **VISITOR'S RELEASE**

The undersigned hereby agrees to hold harmless and indemnify The City of New York, Metropolitan Transportation Authority, New York City Transit Authority, and their respective members, officers, agents and employees, from any and all loss and liability for damages on account of injuries (including death) to persons and damage to property attributable in whole or in part to the negligence of the undersigned while on, or about the premises of the New York City Transit Authority.

4 (#1)

NYCTA Location to be visited: _____1_____

Duration of visit: From ____ A.M.
                          ____ P.M. _____, 198__
                    To   ____ A.M.
                          ____ P.M. _____, 198__ } 2

Reason for visit: _____3_____

Age: __4__ Occupation: __5__

Firm represented: __6__

Employer: __7__

Address of Firm: __8__

Dated: __9__   (Signed) __10__

            Address __11__

Witness: __12__

(Two copies to be signed, one copy for NYCTA, one copy for visitor)

12. Which of the following should be on Line 4? 12.____

   A. 2 P.M.   B. 57
   C. 207th St. Shop   D. 27

13. Which of the following should be on Line 6? 13.____

   A. Joan Sanford
   B. Adam Hart Manufacturing Co.
   C. Oak Point Associates
   D. Patterson Manufacturing Co.

14. Which of the following should be on Line 11? 14.____

   A. 1427 Cedar St., Glendale, N.Y.
   B. 25-16 65th Road, Oak Point, N.Y.
   C. 3961 Tenth Ave., Manhattan, at 207th St.
   D. 26-15 65th Ave., Oak Point, N.Y.

15. Which of the following should be on Line 12? 15._____

    A. Miss Sanford's signature
    B. Mr. Patterson's signature
    C. Paul Jones' signature
    D. Lawrence Austin's name

16. On which of the following lines should *1427 Cedar St., Glendale, N.Y.* be entered? 16._____

    A. 2   B. 3   C. 7   D. 8

17. What is Miss Sanford's occupation? 17._____

    A. Superintendent   B. Protection Agent
    C. Salesperson   D. Manager, Sales

18. Which of the following should be entered in Section 2 of the form? 18._____

    A. 9:00 A.M. and 2:00 P.M.   B. 9:15 A.M. and 2:00 P.M.
    C. 9:15 A.M. and 2:15 P.M.   D. 9:15 A.M. and 3:00 P.M.

19. Six employees drive six passenger cars with Transit Authority decals into the Jamaica Yard parking lot after displaying their passes to the Agent. An hour later, two of those employees drive two of the cars out of the lot. Ten minutes later, two of those employees leave in one of the cars. A half hour after that, the other two employees leave in one of the cars with three other employees seated in the back. 19._____
    How many of the six cars that entered together remain in the lot?

    A. 1   B. 2   C. 3   D. 4

20. *All unusual occurrences and hazards should be reported promptly to the Property Protection Control Desk.* 20._____
    A person on the street throws a rock through the window of the Protection Agent's booth at a train yard, shattering the glass but not causing personal injury. The FIRST action the Protection Agent should take is to

    A. run out to the street and attempt to apprehend the rock thrower
    B. call the Property Protection Control Desk and report the incident
    C. sweep up the broken glass so that no one will step on it
    D. pick up the rock and throw it at the culprit to halt him so he may be apprehended

Questions 21-24.

DIRECTIONS: Questions 21 through 24 are to be answered SOLELY on the basis of the following information.

Under Transit Authority and Property Protection Department rules, only authorized visitors and employees with Authority passes may enter a Transit Authority facility.

21. A woman not employed by the Transit Authority asks a Protection Agent at the East 180th St. train yard whether she may use the yard's ladies room. 21._____
    The Protection Agent should tell her that

    A. she may if she takes no longer than 10 minutes
    B. she must first ask the location chief whether she may use that facility

C. she may do so only if she is related to an employee assigned to the yard
D. he is sorry but Transit Authority rules prohibit her admittance

22. A boy involved in a softball game on a lot next to a bus depot parking lot tells a Protection Agent that one of the batters hit a pitch over the fence and into the Transit Authority lot. He asks permission to retrieve the ball.
Which of the following is the BEST course of action for the Protection Agent?
He should

   A. permit the boy to go onto the lot to retrieve the ball
   B. tell the boy that he may not go onto the lot, but that he can claim the ball at the Transit Authority's Lost Property Office
   C. tell the boy to wait at the gate until he (the Protection Agent) retrieves the ball and returns it to him
   D. tell the boy that he must leave the ball where it landed and that he and his friends must discontinue playing ball so close to the depot parking lot

23. Car Inspector Boggs, employed at the Pitkin Train Yard, calls Agent Hernandez, stationed at an entrance of the train yard, to tell him that his wife, Helen Boggs, is coming to the facility to pick up a personal article from him.
Agent Hernandez should tell Mr. Boggs that

   A. he will have to wait until he returns home to give her the article
   B. he is not permitted to have visitors at the train yard while he is working
   C. he, Agent Hernandez, will call him when his wife arrives and that he must come to the booth to see her
   D. he will send Mrs. Boggs inside to see him

24. A woman with a briefcase enters the lobby at Transit Authority headquarters and is stopped by a Protection Agent assigned there. She says she represents the Fail Safe Brush Company and wants to offer brushes and other home-cleaning products for sale to Transit Authority employees.
The Agent should politely tell her that

   A. she may go to the various floors for that purpose so long as she does not disturb employees while they are working
   B. she first must go to the executive floor to ask the Senior Vice President for permission to solicit employees
   C. she may not enter the building to sell products to Transit Authority employees
   D. if she wishes she may stand in the lobby and solicit employees as they enter or leave the building

25. A Protection Agent on duty at the Jerome Avenue Yard opened the vehicle gate at 2:29 A.M. to allow employee cars with decal numbers 526 and 495 to enter. The car with decal No. 495 was driven out of the yard after having been inside for 37 minutes. The car with decal No. 526 left the yard one hour and 18 minutes after car No. 495.
At what time did car No. 526 leave the yard?

   A. 3:06 A.M.   B. 4:06 A.M.
   C. 4:24 A.M.   D. 4:24 P.M.

Questions 26-29.

DIRECTIONS: Questions 26 through 29 are to be answered SOLELY on the basis of the information in the paragraph below.

    Protection Agent Brown, working the midnight-to-8:00 A.M. tour at the Flushing Bus Depot, discovered a fire at 2:17 A.M. in Bus No. 4651, which was parked in the southeast portion of the depot yard. He turned in an alarm to the Fire Department from Box 3297 on the nearby street at 2:18 A.M. At 2:20 A.M., he called the Property Protection Control Desk and reported the fire and his action to Line Supervisor Wilson. Line Supervisor Wilson instructed Agent Brown to lock his booth and go to the fire alarm box to direct the fire companies. The first arriving companies were Engine 307 and Ladder 154. Brown directed them to the burning bus. Two minutes later, at 2:23 A.M., Battalion Chief Welsh arrived from Battalion 14. The fire had made little headway. It was extinguished in about two minutes. Brown then wrote a fire report for submittal to Line Supervisor Wilson.

26. What was the FIRST thing Protection Agent Brown did after observing the fire?
He

    A. called Battalion Chief Welsh
    B. called the Fire Dispatcher
    C. transmitted an alarm from a nearby alarm box
    D. called 911

27. In what part of the yard was the burning bus?
The

    A. northeast section   B. southwest end
    C. northwest part   D. southeast portion

28. What time did Agent Brown call Line Supervisor Wilson?

    A. 2:18 PM   B. 2:20 AM   C. 2:29 AM   D. 2:36 AM

29. Which of the following CORRECTLY describes the sequence of Agent Brown's actions?
He

    A. saw the fire, turned in an alarm, called the Property Protection Control Desk, directed the fire companies to the fire, and wrote a report
    B. called the Property Protection Control Desk, directed the fire apparatus, directed Chief Welsh, and wrote
    C. a report
    D. called Line Supervisor Wilson, turned in an alarm, waited by the burning bus, and directed the fire companies
    E. called Line Supervisor Wilson, directed the fire fighters, waited for instructions from Line Supervisor Wilson, and wrote a report

Questions 30-31.

DIRECTIONS: Questions 30 and 31 are to be answered SOLELY on the basis of the following paragraph and rule.

    Protection Agents may admit to Transit Authority headquarters only persons with Transit Authority passes, persons with job appointment letters, and persons who have permission to enter from Transit Authority officials.

During his tour in the Authority's headquarters lobby, Protection Agent Williams admitted to the building 326 persons with Authority passes and 41 persons with job appointment letters. He telephoned authorized officials for permission to admit 14 others, 13 of whom were granted permission and entered and one of whom was denied permission. He also turned away two persons who wanted to enter to sell to employees merchandise for their personal use, and one person who appeared inebriated.

30. How many persons did Agent Williams admit to the building? 30.____

    A. 326   B. 367   C. 380   D. 382

31. To how many persons did Agent Williams refuse admittance? 31.____

    A. 4   B. 13   C. 14   D. 41

Questions 32-35.

DIRECTIONS: Questions 32 through 35 are to be answered SOLELY on the basis of the information in the following paragraph.

On Tuesday, October 21, Protection Agent Williams, on duty at the Jamaica Depot, observed a man jump over the fence and into the parking lot at 2:12 P.M. and run to a car that was parked with the engine running. The man, who limped slightly, opened the car door, jumped into the car, and sped, out of the yard. The car was a 1991 gray Buick Electra, license plate 563-JYN, with parking decal No. 6043. The man was white, about 6 feet tall, about 175 pounds, in his mid-20's, with a scar on his left cheek. He wore a blue sportcoat, tan slacks, a white shirt open at the neck with no tie, and brown loafers.

32. What was the color of the car? 32.____

    A. White   B. Blue
    C. Two-tone brown and tan   D. Gray

33. What were the distinguishing personal features of the man who jumped over the fence? 33.____

    A. A scar on the left cheek
    B. Pockmarks on his face
    C. A cast on his left wrist
    D. Bushy eyebrows

34. What was the number on the car's parking decal? 34.____

    A. 1991   B. 673-JYN   C. 6043   D. 175

35. On what day of the week did the incident occur? 35.____

    A. Monday   B. Tuesday   C. Wednesday   D. Sunday

KEY (CORRECT ANSWERS)

1.	C	16.	D
2.	A	17.	C
3.	B	18.	B
4.	C	19.	B
5.	D	20.	B
6.	A	21.	D
7.	A	22.	C
8.	C	23.	C
9.	D	24.	C
10.	C	25.	C
11.	B	26.	C
12.	D	27.	D
13.	B	28.	B
14.	B	29.	A
15.	C	30.	C

31. A
32. D
33. A
34. C
35. B

TEST 2

DIRECTIONS: Each question or incomplete statement is followed by several suggested answers or completions. Select the one that BEST answers the question or completes the statement. *PRINT THE LETTER OF THE CORRECT ANSWER IN THE SPACE AT THE RIGHT.*

Questions 1-10.

DIRECTIONS: Questions 1 through 10 are to be answered SOLELY on the basis of the information in the paragraphs below titled SCRAP TRANSFER and the Record of Scrap Award form.

SCRAP TRANSFER

Protection Agent Robert Green, Pass No. 104123, was assigned to Post 27A at the main entrance of the Fifth Ave., Brooklyn Train Yard on Thursday, October 23, on the 8 A.M.-to-4 P.M. tour. At 10:10 A.M., a scrap removal truck, No. 64, license plate AB-4126, from the J.H. Trucking Company stopped at the gate. The driver showed Agent Green a scrap contract with Award No. 1626 for the removal of 12 headlamps from this location.

Agent Green called Supervisor Raymond Hadley in Storeroom 18 for verification of the award. Supervisor Hadley verified the award. The driver then proceeded to Storeroom 18, where he loaded the headlamps into the truck. Hadley then made out a Materials Permit, signed it, and placed his pass number (521800) on it, and gave it to the driver. At the gate, the driver presented the Materials Permit to Agent Green, who logged out the truck at 10:40 A.M., whereupon the truck left for its destination in the Bronx.

Agent Green transcribed the information on his registry sheet and the Materials Permit to a Record of Scrap Award form, which he handed to Line Supervisor Brian Sullivan (Pass No. 756349), who had just arrived at the post. Line Supervisor Sullivan, after having checked the form carefully, signed it and wrote his pass number on it.

2 (#2)

RECORD OF SCRAP AWARD

DATE _____1_____

POST NO. _____2_____ TOUR _____3_____

NAME OF CARRIER _____4_____ AWARD NO. _____5_____

TRUCK LICENSE NO. _____6_____

TRUCK NO. _____7_____

DESTINATION _____8_____

TIME IN _____9_____ TIME OUT _____10_____

DESCRIPTION OF SCRAP _____11_____

AMOUNT _____12_____

NAME OF SUPERVISOR OR DESIGNEE _____13_____

PASS NUMBER _____

_____14_____ _____15_____
TRANSIT PROPERTY PROTECTION AGENT PASS NO.

_____16_____ _____17_____
LINE SUPERVISOR (SIGNATURE) PASS NO.

1. Which of the following should be on Line 2? 1.____

   A. 27A B. Coney Island
   C. Storeroom 18 D. Main gate

2. Which of the following should be on Line 3? 2.____

   A. 12 Midnight - 8 A.M. B. 12 P.M. - 8 P.M.
   C. 8 A.M. - 4 P.M. D. 4 P.M. - 12 P.M.

3. Which of the following should be on Line 4? 3.____

   A. J.H. Trucking Co. B. Line Supervisor Sullivan
   C. Transit Authority D. Storeroom 18

4. Which of the following should be on Line 8? 4.____

   A. Fifth Ave. Yard B. Bronx, N.Y.
   C. Storeroom 18 D. Post 27A

5. Which of the following should be on Line 10? 5.____

   A. 9:10 A.M. B. 10:10 A.M.
   C. 10:30 A.M. D. 10:40 A.M.

6. Which of the following should be on Line 16?
   _____ signature.
   A. Robert Green's			B. Brian Sullivan's
   C. the truck driver's			D. Raymond Hadley's

7. On which of the following lines should *104123* be entered?
   A. 10		B. 12		C. 15		D. 17

8. On which of the following lines should *AB4216* be entered?
   A. 1		B. 3		C. 6		D. 13

9. On which of the following lines should *12 headlamps* be entered?
   A. 3		B. 11		C. 14		D. 17

10. On which of the following lines should 10:10 A.M. be entered?
    A. 8		B. 9		C. 10		D. 11

Questions 11-15.

DIRECTIONS: Questions 11 through 15 are to be answered SOLELY on the basis of the information in the KEY STATIONS DIRECTORY below. Key Stations are locations which Protection Agents must visit and inspect on their hourly rounds.

KEY STATIONS DIRECTORY

Key Station No. 1 - Protection Agent's booth at Flushing Train Yard
Key Station No. 2 - On parking lot fence adjacent to No. 4 track
Key Station No. 3 - On stairwell No. 8 in the Boiler Room
Key Station No. 4 - On the door leading to the second floor men's locker room
Key Station No. 5 - Alongside the soda machine in the second floor lunchroom
Key Station No. 6 - On the oilhouse door
Key Station No. 7 - Alongside the bulletin board in the main shop
Key Station No. 8 - Next to fire extinguisher No. 12 on the wall to the left of the entrance to the Supervisor's office
Key Station No. 9 - On the bumper block of Track No. 10

11. The number of the key station near the main shop bulletin board is
    A. 5		B. 6		C. 7		D. 8

12. Where is Key Station No. 4?
    A. On the parking lot fence adjacent to Track 4
    B. On the door of the second floor men's locker room
    C. On the oilhouse door
    D. In the second floor lunchroom

13. The number of the key station in the Protection Agent's booth is
    A. 1		B. 3		C. 7		D. 9

14. No. 5 Key Station is located

    A. next to fire extinguisher No. 6 in the Protection Agent's booth
    B. on the bumper block of Track 10
    C. in the second floor lunchroom next to the soda machine
    D. on the parking lot fence near Track No. 4

15. The number of the key station on the parking lot fence adjacent to Track No. 4 is

    A. 1   B. 2   C. 3   D. 8

Questions 16-18.

DIRECTIONS: Questions 16 through 18 are to be answered SOLELY on the basis of the following rule.
A Protection Agent must remain on his post (assigned area) during his entire tour.

16. In order to have lunch, a Protection Agent should

    A. go to the nearest restaurant and eat his lunch quickly
    B. bring his lunch or have another person get his lunch for him
    C. go to his locker room to have a brief lunch
    D. telephone the Property Protection Control Desk to inform the supervisor that he is going for a short lunch break

17. While on duty at a train yard, a Protection Agent discovers that his flashlight, one of the items he is required to have in his possession while he is working, is inoperable.
Which of the following is his BEST course of action?

    A. Go to the nearest hardware store, buy new batteries, a new bulb, or a new flashlight and obtain a receipt.
    B. Go to the location chief's office and borrow a flashlight from an Agent assigned to that office.
    C. Make out a written report stating that the flashlight does not work.
    D. Call the Property Protection Control Desk for a replacement flashlight.

18. A woman in a third floor apartment across the street from a Transit Authority bus depot is standing at the window screaming that her apartment is on fire.
The Protection Agent assigned to the depot, seeing flames behind the woman, should IMMEDIATELY

    A. telephone the Fire Department
    B. lock his booth and rush into the building to rescue the woman
    C. take his fire extinguisher and rush to the apartment to extinguish the flames
    D. run across the street, stand under the window, and call to the woman to jump into his arms

19. Registry Sheets must be filled in by Protection Agents assigned to bus depots, train yards, and certain other Transit Authority locations. A Protection Agent must enter on a Registry Sheet the name and pass number or firm name and address, whichever applies, of each person entering with the time in and time out. For a vehicle, he must enter the vehicle number - if a Transit Authority vehicle, the decal or license number of the vehicle, time in and time out, and the destinations of occupants. Each person enter

ing must sign the Registry Sheet, with the exceptions of Transit Authority Special Inspectors and police officers, who nevertheless must identify themselves to the Protection Agent on duty. The Protection Agent must record the name of the police officer or Special Inspector, his shield number, time of arrival and departure, and car number if the officer or Inspector drove a car onto the property.

If a Transit Authority detective in civilian clothes enters the property, the Protection Agent must

A. allow him to enter the property without asking any questions
B. make sure the detective displays his credentials so that the Protection Agent may record his name, shield number, and time of arrival
C. request the detective to write his name, shield number, and signature upon the Registry Sheet
D. immediately call the location chief to notify him that the detective has been admitted to make an investigation

Questions 20-21.

DIRECTIONS: Questions 20 and 21 are to be answered SOLELY on the basis of the following portion of a rule.

...in the event that a claim is made at a place where a lost article is being held pending transmittal to the Lost Property Office and identification is made to the satisfaction of the employee in charge, such employee may, upon receiving permission from the proper authority, deliver such article to the owner, taking a receipt therefor upon the form prescribed...

20. A Protection Agent at the Flushing bus depot parking lot finds a pair of eyeglasses in a case. Shortly thereafter, a Transit Authority employee states that he dropped the eyeglasses and that his name and address are in the case. He identifies himself and the Protection Agent finds his name and address in the case. A Line Supervisor tells the Protection Agent to have the employee sign a receipt form for the glasses.
What action should the Protection Agent then take?

A. He should tell the employee to try on the glasses and read a sign across the street and a memorandum in small type to prove the glasses are his.
B. He should call the man's supervisor and ask him whether he has seen the employee wearing the glasses the Protection Agent describes.
C. He should immediately give the employee the glasses and allow him to leave with them.
D. He should instruct the employee to sign a receipt form and, after he does so, he should give the employee the glasses.

21. Conductor Alvin Bell finds a briefcase on an *A* train in Brooklyn. He takes it to headquarters at 370 Jay Street at 7:25 P.M. Agent James Norton, on duty there, tells him the Lost Property Office is open only from 8:30 A.M. to 4:30 P.M. Mondays to Fridays. At that moment, a woman enters the lobby and tells Agent Norton that she left a briefcase which contains her name and address and valuable papers on an *A* train. Agent Norton tells her that she will have to return the next business day between 8:30 A.M. and 4:30 P.M. to the Lost Property Office to identify the briefcase.
The information Protection Agent Norton gave the woman was

A. *incorrect* because he should have taken her word for it and should have given her the briefcase immediately
B. *correct* because it might not have been her briefcase
C. *incorrect* because he should have given her the briefcase, with supervisory approval, if she would have identified herself, correctly described the contents of the briefcase, and signed the required receipt
D. *correct* because lost property may be redeemed only at the Lost Property Office

22. *All Protection Agents are required to phone the Property Protection Control Desk between 20 and 40 minutes after the hour, except during the first and last hours of their tours when they are not required to phone in.*
Agent Jane Simlowicz is assigned to Post 14C at the Flushing Train Yard from 8:00 A.M. to 4:00 P.M.
Which of the following times would be appropriate for her to make her first call to the Property Protection Control Desk?

    A. 8:35 AM   B. 9:35 AM   C. 9:50 AM   D. 10:45 AM

23. *The playing of musical instruments on Transit Authority property is forbidden.*
During his lunch period, a Transit Authority employee begins playing a bagpipe in a bus depot parking lot to practice his part with a Transit Authority contingent in the Saint Patrick's Day Parade.
The Protection Agent on duty should tell the employee to

    A. play the bagpipe softly at the far end of the parking lot
    B. return to the garage to get his supervisor's permission to practice on the bagpipe in the parking lot
    C. enter a bus parked in the lot, close the doors, and play the bagpipe so it cannot be heard outside
    D. stop playing the bagpipe

24. Agent Fitzgerald, on duty at the bus depot, observes a woman employee come out of the bus garage and enter a car parked on the depot's lot. The car bursts into flames when she turns the ignition key.
The FIRST thing Agent Fitzgerald should consider doing is to

    A. run to the nearest fire alarm box and transmit an alarm
    B. call the Property Protection Control Desk and ask a supervisor to summon the Fire Department
    C. run to the car and try to open the door and pull the woman to safety
    D. rush into the depot, get a pail of water, and throw the water onto the burning car

25. *Telephones in Transit Authority buildings and in other Transit Authority facilities are solely for the business of the Transit Authority.*
A man enters the lobby of the Transit Authority building at 25 Chapel Street and tells the Agent on duty that his car has been struck by another vehicle and that he wants to telephone for a tow truck.
The Agent should tell him that

    A. he may go to one of the upper floors and ask a Transit Authority employee whether he may use that employee's telephone
    B. he should go to the corner of Jay Street and use the police emergency telephone that is on the lamppost

C. he is sorry but all Transit Authority telephones are for Transit Authority business calls only
D. he, the Protection Agent, will call 911 and ask the police to send a tow truck

Questions 26-30.

DIRECTIONS: Questions 26 through 30 are to be answered SOLELY on the basis of the information in the following table.

ASSIGNMENTS FOR THE WEEK OF OCTOBER 19

Title & Name	Post	Tour	Off
Protection Agent John Hall	2B	5 PM - 1 AM	Tues. & Wed.
Protection Agent William Ball	10A	8 AM - 4 PM	Thurs. & Fri.
Protection Agent Robert Hale	4A	4 PM - 12 PM	Sat. & Sun.
Protection Agent Sandra Hill	3B	12 PM - 8 AM	Fri. & Sat.
Protection Agent Brenda Wall	11C	7 PM - 3 AM	Wed. & Thurs.

26. The tour of 4 P.M. to Midnight with Friday and Saturday off is worked by

    A. Robert Hale   B. Brenda Wall
    C. William Ball   D. none of the Agents

27. Which Agent has Saturday and Sunday off?

    A. John Hall   B. Robert Hale
    C. Brenda Wall   D. Sandra Hill

28. What day of the week do all the Agents work?

    A. Monday   B. Wednesday   C. Thursday   D. Sunday

29. Which of the Agents are off on Wednesday?

    A. Ball and Wall   B. Hall and Hale
    C. Wall and Hall   D. Hill and Ball

30. Which of the Agents works Saturday through Wednesday?

    A. Sandra Hill   B. John Hall
    C. William Ball   D. Brenda Wall

31. *Only authorized employees are permitted to enter a Protection Agent's booth.*
A woman with a boy about 4 years old approaches the Agent on duty at the 207th St. Yard on Easter Sunday and asks whether she may leave her son in the booth for about a half hour while she visits a seriously ill bedridden friend across the street. The Agent should tell her

    A. that since her son is not an authorized employee, he cannot enter the booth
    B. the boy may sit in the booth for no longer than a half hour so long as he is quiet and does not touch any property
    C. she should take the boy to the nearest police precinct and pick him up upon her return
    D. she should take the boy to a day care center where experienced children's counselors will care for him

32. While on duty at the Jamaica Yard, Agent Barbara McCoy sees a man fall in the yard and lie motionless, apparently the victim of a heart attack.
    Which of the following actions should she take FIRST?

    A. Lift the man and take him into the Protection Agent's booth.
    B. Write a report of an unusual occurrence.
    C. Call 911 and ask for an ambulance.
    D. Go to the yard supervisor and ask him to assign personnel to drive the man to a hospital.

33. *Employees are prohibited from possessing or drinking alcoholic beverages on Transit Authority property.*
    An Authority employee assigned to the 207th St. Main Shop is about to retire, and his co-workers have planned a farewell party. Some buy food, soda, coffee, and tea at a nearby supermarket and take it into the yard. Agent Simmons, on duty at the entrance booth, inspects their bundles and allows them to enter. Another of the retiree's co-workers carries a bag containing a bottle of Scotch and a bottle of rye.
    Agent Simmons, after inspecting the bag, should tell him

    A. to make sure that none of the contents are spilled on the floor of the party room
    B. to make sure that neither of the bottles get broken
    C. to make sure that the empty bottles and other trash are disposed of properly
    D. that he cannot take the contents of the bag onto Authority property

34. *Transit Authority employees are required to present a Materials Pass before being permitted to take any Authority material or personal property from Transit Authority property.*
    James Thompson, a Farebox Maintainer, is carrying a package as he exits from his work location. The Agent on duty asks him for a Materials Pass. Mr. Thompson opens the package and displays a large box of cigars. What action should the Protection Agent take?
    He should

    A. allow the employee to leave with the cigars since they are not Transit Authority material
    B. call Mr. Thompson's supervisor to ask whether Mr. Thompson may take the cigars with him
    C. tell Mr. Thompson that he may take the cigars with him only if he produces a sales slip for them
    D. explain to Mr. Thompson that he must obtain a Materials Pass before he can take the package out of the facility

35. *Each Protection Agent who is assigned to a post where a watchclock is required must take every precaution to protect the watchclock from damage and theft. It must never be dropped or abused in any way. The Agent is held strictly accountable for any damage to the clock during his tour. Therefore, he must examine the clock and its case carefully in the presence of the Agent he relieves and report any irregularity immediately to the Property Protection Control Desk.*
    If, upon arrival for duty, a Protection Agent finds that the watchclock has been damaged, his FIRST action should be to

A. accept full responsibility for the damage
B. lock up the watchclock as a precaution against theft
C. report the finding to the Property Protection Control Desk
D. tell the Agent on duty that he cannot relieve him because he has apparently dropped or abused the watchclock

---

KEY (CORRECT ANSWERS)

1.	A	16.	B
2.	C	17.	D
3.	A	18.	A
4.	B	19.	B
5.	D	20.	D
6.	B	21.	C
7.	C	22.	B
8.	C	23.	D
9.	B	24.	C
10.	B	25.	C
11.	C	26.	D
12.	B	27.	B
13.	A	28.	A
14.	C	29.	C
15.	B	30.	C

31. A
32. C
33. D
34. D
35. C

EXAMINATION SECTION
TEST 1

DIRECTIONS: Each question or incomplete statement is followed by several suggested answers or completions. Select the one that *BEST* answers the question or completes the statement. *PRINT THE LETTER OF THE CORRECT ANSWER IN THE SPACE AT THE RIGHT.*

1. When a security officer fails to report to work in time to make his scheduled relief, the security officer on duty must call the foreman immediately.
   The *MAIN* reason for this procedure is to

   A. make sure that the security officer on duty is not overworked
   B. make a record of the number of times that a security officer is late
   C. make sure that Authority property and materials are continuously guarded
   D. prevent the security officer who is late from being paid for the time that he did not work

   1.____

2. A security officer must report to his foreman any employee who is on Authority property in an intoxicated condition.
   The *MAIN* reason for this procedure is that

   A. this employee may give the general public the impression that many Authority employees drink while on duty
   B. an employee who drinks on the job may encourage fellow employees to also drink on the job
   C. an intoxicated employee may endanger himself and other Authority employees
   D. the intoxicated employee's foreman may not have noticed this condition

   2.____

3. If a security officer is required to make hourly calls to his foreman within twenty minutes of the hour, a correct time for a security officer to make his hourly call is at

   A. 3:36 A.M.   B. 8:29 A.M.   C. 4:27 A.M.   D. 7:48 P.M.

   3.____

4. Which of the following characteristics of a security officer doing record keeping is *MOST* important?

   A. Familiarity with rules and procedures
   B. An analytical mind
   C. Accuracy
   D. Speed

   4.____

5. Of the following, the type of equipment that a security officer working a 12:00 midnight to 8:00 A.M. shift would be expected to use *MOST* often is a

   A. pistol   B. flashlight   C. camera   D. siren

   5.____

6. Before going on duty, a security officer is required to read all new bulletins posted on the bulletin board. The *MAIN* reason for this requirement is to

   A. acquaint the security officer with new regulations
   B. make sure that the security officer understands all the rules
   C. make the security officer responsible for any violations of the rules
   D. acquaint the security officer with his rights

   6.____

7. Assume that soon after being appointed as a security officer, you decide that some of the rules and regulations of the Authority are unwise.
Of the following, you should

   A. disregard these rules and regulations and use your own good judgment
   B. not do your job until some changes are made
   C. make the changes that you decide are necessary
   D. carry out these rules and regulations regardless of your opinion

Questions 8-11.
DIRECTIONS: Questions 8 to 11 are based on information contained in LOCATION OF KEY STATIONS shown below. When answering these questions, refer to this information.

LOCATION OF KEY STATIONS

No. 12 key station - located on double fire exit door adjacent to Briarcliff Avenue vehicle ramp.
No. 13 key station - located on wall adjacent to fire exit door in Unit Repair Section.
No. 14 key station - located in men's locker room on door leading to washroom near water cooler.
No. 15 key station - located in corridor leading to transportation area on wall adjacent to room number 1 and opposite to first aid room.
No. 16 key station - located on wall adjacent to door leading into unit storeroom.
No. 17 key station - located on a wall adjacent to double fire exit doors in Unit Repair Section.
No. 18 key station - located on wall adjacent to fire exit door in body shop.

8. Two key stations are located on or near double fire exit doors. One of them is key station No. 12.
The *other* is key station No.

   A. 13   B. 14   C. 17   D. 18

9. If a security officer took a drink of water, he would MOST likely do so at a location closest to key station No.

   A. 12   B. 14   C. 16   D. 17

10. A delivery of $759.00 worth of supplies would MOST likely be made to a location which is closest to key station No.

    A. 13   B. 14   C. 16   D. 18

11. A fire exit door will NOT be found at key station No.

    A. 12   B. 13   C. 15   D. 17

12. When preparing a report, a security officer should generally make *at least* one extra copy so that

    A. it can be sent to a newspaper
    B. there will be no mistakes made
    C. a personal record can be kept
    D. the information in the report can be discussed by all other security officers

13. In writing a report about a storeroom robbery by several men, the LEAST important of the following information is

   A. the number of men involved
   B. a list of the items that were stolen
   C. how the men entered the storeroom
   D. how many lights were left on by the robbers

Questions 14-19.

DIRECTIONS: Questions 14 to 19 are based on the paragraph REGISTRY SHEETS shown below. When answering these questions, refer to this paragraph.

REGISTRY SHEETS

Where registry sheets are in effect, the security officer must legibly print Authority employee's pass number, title, license and vehicle number, destination, time in and time out; and each Authority employee must sign his or her name. The same procedure is to be applied to visitors, except in place of a pass number each visitor will indicate his address or firm name; and visitors must also sign waivers. Information is to be obtained from driver's license, firm credential card, or any other appropriate identification, All visitors must state their purpose for entering upon the property. If they desire to visit anyone, verification must be made before entry is permitted. All persons signing sheet must sign in when entering upon the property, and sign out again when leaving. The security officer will, at the end of his tour, draw a horizontal line across the entire sheet after his last entry, indicating the end of one tour and the beginning of another. At the top of each sheet the security officer will enter the number of entries made during his tour, the sheet number, post, and date. Sheets are to begin with number 1 on the first day of the month, and should be kept in numerical order. Each security officer will read the orders at each post to see whether any changes are made and at which hours control sheets are in effect.

14. Waivers need NOT be signed by

   A. Authority employees   B. vendors
   C. reporters   D. salesmen

15. All visitors are required to state

   A. whether they have a criminal record
   B. the reason for their visit
   C. the reason they are not bonded
   D. whether they have ever worked for the Authority

16. In the paragraph, the statement is made that "verification must be made before entry is permitted." The word *verification* means, most nearly,

   A. allowance   B. confirmation   C. refusal   D. disposal

17. A security officer must draw a horizontal line across the entire registry sheet in order to show that

   A. he is being replaced to check a disturbance outside
   B. the last tour for the day has been completed
   C. one tour is ending and another is beginning
   D. a visitor has finished his business and is leaving

18. At the top of a registry sheet, it is NOT necessary for a security officer to list the

    A. tour number
    B. number of entries made
    C. sheet number
    D. date

19. A security officer should check at which hours control sheets are in effect by reading

    A. registry sheet number 1, on the first day of each month
    B. the orders at each post
    C. the time in and time out that each person has entered on the registry sheet
    D. the last entry made on the registry sheet used before the start of his tour

20. Assume that after working as a security officer for some time, your foreman is replaced by a new foreman.
    If this new foreman insists on explaining to you the procedure for doing a job which you know how to do very well, you should listen to the new foreman MAINLY because

    A. you may catch him in an error and thus prove you know your job
    B. it is wise to humor a foreman even when he is wrong
    C. you can do the job the way you like after the foreman leaves
    D. it will be your responsibility to perform the job the way the new foreman wants it done

21. All security officers are instructed that whenever they report an accident to the main office by telephone, prior to preparing their written accident report, they should request the name of the person receiving the call and also make a note of the time.
    The MAIN purpose of this precaution is to fix responsibility for the

    A. cause of the accident
    B. recording of the accident at the main office
    C. accuracy of the accident report
    D. preparation of the written report

22. One of your duties as a security officer will be to compile the facts about an accident in a written report. The LEAST important item to include in such an accident report is

    A. the people involved
    B. what action you took
    C. the extent of personal injuries
    D. why you think the accident happened

23. It is MOST important for a written report to be

    A. accurate
    B. brief
    C. detailed
    D. properly punctuated

24. In a large bus shop where many security officers are used, each security officer is required to do his work in a definite prescribed manner MAINLY because

    A. this practice insures discipline
    B. no other method will work
    C. this practice will keep the security officer from being inattentive on the job
    D. there will be less need for the security officers to consult with their supervisors

25. When an unusual situation arises on the job, and it would take too long for you to contact your foreman for advice, the *BEST* procedure for you to follow is to

    A. play it safe and take no action
    B. confer with another security officer
    C. check your rule book for the proper procedure
    D. act according to your best judgment

26. At the scene of an accident it is good first-aid procedure to treat the most badly injured person first. Of the following injured people, the person *LEAST* in need of immediate care is one who

    A. is bleeding rapidly
    B. finds great difficulty in breathing
    C. appears to have sprained an ankle
    D. complains of severe pains in his chest

Questions 27-32.

DIRECTIONS: Questions 27 to 32 are based on the paragraph THEFT shown below. When answering these questions, refer to this paragraph.

THEFT

A security officer must be alert at all times to discourage the willful removal of property and material of the Authority by individuals for self gain. Should a security officer detect such an individual, he should detain him and immediately call the supervisor at that location. No force should be used during the process of detainment. However, should the individual bolt from the premises, the security officer will be expected to offer some clues for his apprehension. Therefore, he should try to remember some characteristic traits about the individual, such as clothing, height, coloring, speech, and how he made his approach. Unusual characteristics such as a scar or a limp are most important. If a car is used, the security officer should take the license plate number of said car. Above information should be supplied to the responding peace officer and the special inspection control desk. In desolate locations, the security officer should first call the police and then the special inspection control desk. Any security officer having information of the theft should contact the director of special inspection by telephone or by mail. This information will be kept confidential if desired.

27. A security officer is required to be attentive on the job at all times, *MAINLY* to

    A. get as much work done as possible
    B. prevent the stealing of Authority property
    C. show his supervisor that he is doing a good job
    D. prevent any other security officer from patrolling the area to which he is assigned

28. In the second sentence, the word *detain* means, most nearly,

    A. delay   B. avoid   C. call   D. report

29. The prescribed course of action a security officer should take when he discovers a person stealing Authority property is to

    A. make sure that all gates are closed to prevent the thief from escaping
    B. detain the thief and quickly call the supervisor

C. use his club to keep the thief there until the police arrive
D. call another security officer for assistance

30. The MOST useful of the following descriptions of a runaway thief would be that he is a

    A. tall man who runs fast
    B. man with blue eyes
    C. man with black hair
    D. tall man who limps

31. The license plate number of a car which is used by a thief to escape should be reported by & security officer to the responding peace officer *and* the

    A. director of protection agents
    B. security officer's supervisor
    C. special inspection control desk
    D. department of motor vehicles

32. A security officer patrolling a desolate area has spotted a thief. The security officer should FIRST call

    A. his supervisor
    B. the police
    C. the special inspection control desk
    D. the director of special inspection

33. It is very important that Authority officials be given legible hand-written reports on unusual occurrences if there is no time to type them up.
    According to the above statement about hand-written reports, it would be MOST useful if a security officer, when writing a report,

    A. did not write on the back of the page
    B. did not use big words
    C. wrote concisely
    D. wrote out all the information clearly

34. A security officer sees a youth marking up the wall surrounding Authority property. He should FIRST

    A. tell the youth to stop
    B. arrest the youth
    C. call a policeman
    D. punish the youth

35. If an alarm goes off and a security officer observes a van speeding away from a storeroom, the information that would be LEAST helpful in identifying the van would be the

    A. color of the van
    B. approximate speed at which the van passed his post
    C. state and the license plate number of the van
    D. manufacturer and model of the van

36. A security officer notices that a power line, knocked down by a storm, has electrified a steel flagpole. After notifying his supervisor, of the following it would be BEST to

    A. put a wooden "caution" sign on the flagpole and call the Fire Department
    B. remove the wire from the flagpole
    C. stay near the flagpole and warn everyone not to go near the flagpole
    D. say nothing about it until his supervisor arrives

37. Another Authority employee informs a security officer, who is on duty at the entrance to an Authority bus depot, that he has found a bomb in the locker room. The security officer should FIRST

    A. investigate to see if it is actually a bomb
    B. clear the area of persons in or near the locker room
    C. question the man closely to determine if he really saw a bomb
    D. call the Bomb Squad for instructions on handling bombs

38. In MOST cases, a written report on an accident is better than an oral report because a written report

    A. can be referred to later
    B. takes less time to prepare
    C. includes more of the facts
    D. reduces the number of court cases

39. A report of an accident is MOST likely to be accurate if written by the security officer

    A. long after the event
    B. after taking about a week to make sure he has all the facts
    C. immediately after the event
    D. after thoroughly discussing the event with others for several days

40. The gross weight of a carton and its contents is 830.2 pounds. If the weight of the carton alone is 98.7 pounds, the net weight of the contents of the carton is

    A. 731.5 pounds   B. 732.5 pounds
    C. 741.5 pounds   D. 831.5 pounds

KEY (CORRECT ANSWERS)

1. C	11. C	21. B	31. C
2. C	12. C	22. D	32. B
3. D	13. D	23. A	33. D
4. C	14. A	24. D	34. A
5. B	15. B	25. D	35. B
6. A	16. B	26. C	36. C
7. D	17. C	27. B	37. B
8. C	18. A	28. A	38. A
9. B	19. B	29. B	39. C
10. C	20. D	30. D	40. A

TEST 2

DIRECTIONS: Each question or incomplete statement is followed by several suggested answers or completions. Select the one that *BEST* answers the question or completes the statement. *PRINT THE LETTER OF THE CORRECT ANSWER TN THE SPACE AT THE RIGHT.*

Questions 1-10.

DIRECTIONS: Read the DESCRIPTION OF ACCIDENT carefully. Then answer Questions 1 to 10, inclusive, using only this information in picking your answer.

DESCRIPTION OF ACCIDENT

On Friday, May 9th, at about 2:30 p.m, Bus Operator Joe Able, badge no, 1234, was operating his half-filled bus, Authority no. 5678, northbound along Fifth Ave., when a green Ford truck, N.Y. license no. 9012, driven by Sam Wood, came out of an Authority storeroom entrance into the path of the bus. To avoid hitting the truck, Joe Able turned his steering wheel sharply to the left, causing his bus to cross the solid white line into the opposite lane where the bus crashed head-on into a black 1975 Mercury, N.Y. license no. 3456, driven by Bill Green. The crash caused the Mercury to sideswipe a blue VW, N.J. license 7890, driven by Jim White, which was double-parked while he made a delivery. The sudden movement of the bus caused one of the passengers, Mrs. Jane Smith, to fall, striking her head on one of the seats, Joe Able blew his horn vigorously to summon aid and Security Officer Fred Norton, badge no. 9876, and Stockman Al Blue, badge no. 5432, came out of the storeroom and rendered assistance. While Norton gave Mrs. Smith first aid, Blue summoned an ambulance for Green. A tow truck removed Green's car and Able found that the bus could operate under its own power, so he returned to the garage.

1. The Ford truck was driven by
   A. Able B. Green C. Wood D. White

2. The Authority no. of the bus was
   A. 1234 B. 5678 C. 9012 D. 3456

3. The bus was driven by
   A. Able B. Green C. Wood D. White

4. The license no. of the VW was
   A. 9012 B. 3456 C. 7890 D. 5432

5. The horn of the bus summoned
   A. Blue B. Green C. White D. Smith

6. The badge no. of the security officer was
   A. 5432 B. 5678 C. 1234 D. 9876

7. The Mercury was driven by
   A. Smith B. Norton C. White D. Green

8. The bus was traveling

   A. North   B. East   C. South   D. West

9. The vehicle towed away was a

   A. bus   B. Ford   C. Mercury   D. VW

10. Mrs. Smith hurt her

    A. head   B. back   C. arm   D. leg

11. If more than one security officer is involved in an incident, each is required to write a report giving his version of what happened. By having *both* reports submitted, the information gathered

    A. should be more complete
    B. should clear the Authority from any blame
    C. cannot be disputed
    D. will not be opinionated

12. If a security officer gets $5.42 per hour, and $8.13 per hour for overtime work, his *gross* salary for a week in which he works 5 hours over his regular 40 hours is

    A. $216.80   B. $243.90   C. $257.45   D. $325.20

13. It takes 2 min. 45 sec. for a security officer to travel to his first clock station, 3 min. to get to the second, 2 min. to get to the third, 5 1/2 min. to get to the fourth, and 4 min. 15 sec. to get from the fourth back to the starting point.
    Neglecting the time spent at each clock station, the *TOTAL* time needed to make one round tour is

    A. 16 min. 45 sec.   B. 17 min. 15 sec.
    C. 17 min. 30 sec.   D. 18 min.

Questions 14-20.

DIRECTIONS: Questions 14 to 20 are based on the rules listed below and are numbered 1 to 7. Each question gives a situation in which a security officer has disobeyed at least one rule. For each question, select from among the four choices the number of a rule which the security officer has disobeyed.

Rule Number 1: A security officer is subject to the orders of foremen (security officer) and of employees assigned to the special inspection control desk.

Rule Number 2: A security officer must protect system properties against fire, theft, vandalism, and unauthorized entrance.

Rule Number 3: A security officer is responsible for all equipment and other property entrusted to him and must see that such equipment is kept in good condition.

Rule Number 4: A security officer must give information about an accident only to authorized Authority officials.

Rule Number 5: A security officer must be attired in the prescribed uniform with badge displayed at all times while on duty.

Rule Number 6: A security officer must remain on duty during his entire tour and must therefore eat lunch on the job.

Rule Number 7: A security officer must not allow another employee to perform any part of his duties without proper authority.

14. While investigating a noise in the parking lot at night, Security Officer Johnson could not see very well because his flashlight was not in working order. Johnson disobeyed Rule Number

    A. 1   B. 3   C. 5   D. 7

15. Without getting permission to do so, Security Officer Simpson went to the locker room to get his lunch and let the porter, Baxter, check the credentials of a truck driver whose truck was about to enter Authority property. Simpson disobeyed Rule Number

    A. 1   B. 3   C. 5   D. 7

16. After being told by his foreman to check the door of Storeroom No. 15 before leaving, Security Officer Roscoe went off duty before seeing whether or not the door was properly locked. Roscoe disobeyed Rule Number

    A. 1   B. 4   C. 6   D. 7

17. Security Officer Andrews removed his badge ten minutes before going off duty. Andrews disobeyed Rule Number

    A. 2   B. 4   C. 5   D. 6

18. Security Officer Paul left his post inside the train yard in order to make a personal telephone call. As a result, Paul disobeyed Rule Number

    A. 2   B. 4   C. 5   D. 7

19. Security Officer Burroughs gave a newspaper reporter details of an accident that occurred on his post. Burroughs disobeyed Rule Number

    A. 1   B. 2   C. 3   D. 4

20. Security Officer Grenich left his post unattended and went across the street to a diner, since he left his lunch at home. Grenich disobeyed Rule Number

    A. 4   B. 5   C. 6   D. 7

Questions 21-25.

DIRECTIONS: Questions 21 to 25 are based on the UNUSUAL OCCURRENCE REPORT given below. Five phrases in the report have been removed and are listed below the report as 1. through 5. In each of the five places where phrases of the report have been left out, the number of a question has been inserted. For each question, select the number of the missing phrase which would make the report read correctly.

UNUSUAL OCCURRENCE REPORT

Post 20A
Tour 12 a.m.-8 a.m.
Date August 13

Location of Occurrence: Storeroom #55

REMARKS: While making rounds this morning I thought that I heard some strange sounds coming from Storeroom #55. Upon investigation, I saw that 21 and that the door to the storeroom was slightly opened. At 2:45 a.m. I 22 .

Suddenly two men jumped out from 23 , dropped the tools which they were holding, and made a dash for the door. I ordered them to stop, but they just kept running.

I was able to get a good look at both of them. One man was wearing a green jacket and had a full beard and the other was short and had blond hair. Immediately, I called the police and about two minutes later I notified 24 . I 25 the police arrived and I gave them the complete details of the incident.

Security Officer Donald Rimson 23807
Signature Pass No.

1. the special inspection control desk
2. behind some crates
3. the lock had been tampered with
4. remained at the storeroom until
5. entered the storeroom and began to look around

21. A. 1   B. 3   C. 4   D. 5
22. A. 2   B. 3   C. 4   D. 5
23. A. 1   B. 2   C. 3   D. 4
24. A. 1   B. 2   C. 3   D. 4
25. A. 2   B. 3   C. 4   D. 5

26. Employees using supplies from a first-aid kit are generally required to submit an immediate report on what happened and what supplies were used.
Of the following, the MOST important reason for this regulation is to

   A. make sure that supplies which are used are replaced
   B. prevent theft
   C. see that the correct employee gets credit for taking action
   D. identify the person who last used the kit

27. The log book of a security officer stationed at an entry gate shows 47 entries in two hours. At this rate, the number of entries in eight hours is

   A. 108   B. 168   C. 188   D. 376

28. A truck driver leaving Authority property has a requisition form showing 14 cartons of pencils, 12 cartons of pens, 27 cartons of envelopes, and 39 cartons of writing pads. If an actual count of the cartons on the truck shows only 77 cartons, the number of cartons missing is

   A. 15   B. 14   C. 12   D. 5

29. It is NOT advisable to move an injured man before the arrival of a doctor if the man has

    A. a severe nosebleed
    B. burns over 3% of his body
    C. fainted from the heat
    D. possibly injured his spine

30. While making rounds during daylight hours, a security officer notices that one of the floodlights in the parking lot has been left on. The security officer should

    A. turn the light off because it will cost him his job if his foreman finds out about this
    B. turn the light off, because it is not needed
    C. leave the light on and call his foreman to investigate
    D. leave the light on to make it easier for him to see anything which looks suspicious

31. A security officer comes upon an empty fire extinguisher while making his rounds. Of the following, it is MOST important that he

    A. ignore it, since mentioning this might get someone into trouble
    B. make a note not to use that extinguisher in case of a fire
    C. report it to the next security officer who relieves him
    D. report it to his foreman

32. The windows of the booth used by a security officer must be kept clean and clear of any obstructions at all times. The MOST obvious reason for this is to

    A. enable anyone passing by the booth to look into it and see who is on duty
    B. allow as much daylight as possible to enter the booth so that a security officer can conserve electricity by keeping booth lights turned off
    C. enable a security officer to see what is happening outside of the booth
    D. make certain that a security officer makes a good impression on inspectors who are passing by the booth

33. A security officer must be completely familiar with door schedules (when the door must be locked and when open), particularly during hours when employees are reporting for work.
    If a security officer does not know all door schedules for his post it would be BEST for him to

    A. quickly get a copy of the door schedule from the security officer who will relieve him
    B. check the bulletin board at a nearby post to see if he can get a copy of the door schedules
    C. let his foreman know about it immediately, so the foreman can give him the information he needs
    D. check the rules and regulations book for the information

Questions 34-37.

DIRECTIONS: Questions 34 to 37 inclusive are based on the paragraph FIRE FIGHTING shown below. When answering these questions, refer to this paragraph.

FIRE FIGHTING

A security officer should remember the cardinal rule that water or soda acid fire extinguishers should not be used on any electrical fire, and apply it in the case of a fire near the third rail. In addition, security officers should familiarize themselves with all available fire alarms and fire-fighting equipment within their assigned posts. Use of the fire alarm should bring responding Fire Department apparatus quickly to the scene. Familiarity with the fire-fighting equipment near his post would help in putting out incipient fires. Any man calling for the Fire Department should remain outside so that he can direct the Fire Department to the fire. As soon as possible thereafter, the special inspection desk must be notified and a complete written report of the fire, no matter how small, must be submitted to this office. The security officer must give the exact time and place it started, who discovered it, how it was extinguished, the damage done, cause of same, list of any injured persons with the extent of their injuries, and the name of the Fire Chief in charge. All defects noticed by the security officer concerning the fire alarm or any firefighting equipment must be reported to the special inspection department.

34. It would be proper to use water to put out a fire in a(n)

    A. electric motor
    B. electric switch box
    C. waste paper trash can
    D. electric generator

35. After calling the Fire Department from a street box to report a fire, the security officer should then

    A. return to the fire and help put it out
    B. stay outside and direct the Fire Department to the fire
    C. find a phone and call his boss
    D. write out a report for the special inspection desk

36. A security officer is required to submit a complete written report of a fire

    A. two weeks after the fire
    B. the day following the fire
    C. as soon as possible
    D. at his convenience

37. In his report of a fire, it is *NOT* necessary for the security officer to state

    A. time and place of the fire
    B. who discovered the fire
    C. the names of persons injured
    D. quantity of Fire Department equipment used

38. While making afternoon rounds, a security officer climbs a stairway which has a loose banister.
    To avoid having someone injured, the security officer should

    A. inform his foreman of the hazard so that it can be corrected
    B. fix the banister himself, since it can probably be fixed quickly
    C. block the stairway with rope at the top and bottom so that no one else can use it
    D. put up a caution sign in the hallway leading to the stairway

39. If, while on duty, a security officer sees an accident which results in injuries to Authority employees, it would be most important for him to FIRST

   A. render all possible first-aid to the injured
   B. record the exact time the accident happened
   C. write out an accident report
   D. try to find out what caused the accident

40. If a security officer has many accidents, no matter what shift or location he is assigned to, the MOST likely reason for this is

   A. lack of safety devices
   B. not enough safety posters
   C. inferior equipment and materials
   D. careless work practices

KEY (CORRECT ANSWERS)

1.	C	11.	A	21.	B	31.	D
2.	B	12.	C	22.	D	32.	C
3.	A	13.	C	23.	B	33.	C
4.	C	14.	B	24.	A	34.	C
5.	A	15.	D	25.	C	35.	B
6.	D	16.	A	26.	A	36.	C
7.	D	17.	C	27.	C	37.	D
8.	A	18.	A	28.	A	38.	A
9.	C	19.	D	29.	D	39.	A
10.	A	20.	C	30.	B	40.	D

EXAMINATION SECTION
TEST 1

DIRECTIONS: Each question or incomplete statement is followed by several suggested answers or completions. Select the one that BEST answers the question or completes the statement. *PRINT THE LETTER OF THE CORRECT ANSWER IN THE SPACE AT THE RIGHT.*

1. The officer who investigates accidents is always required to make a complete and accurate report.
Of the following, the BEST reason for this procedure is to

   A. protect the operating agency against possible false claims
   B. provide a file of incidents which can be used as basic material for an accident prevention campaign
   C. provide the management with concrete evidence of violations of the rules by employees
   D. indicate what repairs need to be made

2. It is suggested that an officer keep all persons away from the area of an accident until an investigation has been completed.
This suggested procedure is

   A. *good;* witnesses will be more likely to agree on a single story
   B. *bad;* such action blocks traffic flow and causes congestion
   C. *good;* objects of possible use as evidence will be protected from damage or loss
   D. *bad;* the flow of normal pedestrian traffic provides an opportunity for an investigator to determine the cause of the accident

3. A man having business with your agency is arguing with you and accuses you of being prejudiced against him. Although you explain to him that this is not so, he demands to see your supervisor.
Of the following, the BEST course of action for you to take is to

   A. continue arguing with him until you have worn him out or convinced him
   B. take him to your supervisor
   C. ignore him and walk away from him to another part of the office
   D. escort him out of the office

4. An officer receives instructions from his supervisor which he does not fully understand.
For the officer to ask for a further explanation would be

   A. *good;* chiefly because his supervisor will be impressed with his interest in his work
   B. *poor;* chiefly because the time of the supervisor will be needlessly wasted
   C. *good;* chiefly because proper performance depends on full understanding of the work to be done
   D. *poor;* chiefly because officers should be able to think for themselves

5. A person is making a complaint to an officer which seems unreasonable and of little importance.
Of the following, the BEST action for the officer to take is to

A. criticize the person making the complaint for taking up his valuable time
B. laugh over the matter to show that the complaint is minor and silly
C. tell the person that anyone responsible for his grievance will be prosecuted
D. listen to the person making the complaint and tell him that the matter will be investigated

6. A member of the department shall not indulge in intoxicating liquor while in uniform. A member of the department is not required to wear a uniform, and a uniformed member while out of uniform shall not indulge in intoxicants to an extent unfitting him for duty.
Of the following, the MOST correct interpretation of this rule is that a

A. member, off duty, not in uniform, may drink intoxicating liquor
B. member, not on duty, but in uniform, may drink intoxicating liquor
C. member, on duty, in uniform, may drink intoxicants
D. uniformed member, in civilian clothes, may not drink intoxicants

7. You have a suggestion for an important change which you believe will improve a certain procedure in your agency. Of the following, the next course of action for you to take is to

A. try it out yourself
B. submit the suggestion to your immediate supervisor
C. write a letter to the head of your agency asking for his approval
D. wait until you are asked for suggestions before submitting this one

8. An officer shall study maps and literature concerning his assigned area and the streets and points of interest nearby.
Of the following, the BEST reason for this rule is that

A. the officer will be better able to give correct information to persons desiring it
B. the officer will be better able to drive a vehicle in the area
C. the officer will not lose interest in his work
D. supervisors will not need to train the officers in this subject

9. In asking a witness to a crime to identify a suspect, it is a common practice to place the suspect with a group of persons and ask the witness to pick out the person in question.
Of the following, the BEST reason for this practice is that it will

A. make the identification more reliable than if the witness were shown the suspect alone
B. protect the witness against reprisals
C. make sure that the witness is telling the truth
D. help select other participants in the crime at the same time

10. It is most important for all officers to obey the "Rules and Regulations" of their agency.
Of the following, the BEST reason for this statement is that

A. supervisors will not need to train their new officers
B. officers will never have to use their own judgment
C. uniform procedures will be followed
D. officers will not need to ask their supervisors for assistance

Questions 11-13.

DIRECTIONS: Answer questions 11 to 13 SOLELY on the basis of the following paragraph.

All members of the police force must recognize that the people, through their representatives, hire and pay the police and that, as in any other employment, there must exist a proper employer-employee relationship. The police officer must understand that the essence of a correct police attitude is a willingness to serve, but at the same time, he should distinguish between service and servility, and between courtesy and softness. He must be firm but also courteous, avoiding even an appearance of rudeness. He should develop a position that is friendly and unbiased, pleasant and sympathetic, in his relations with the general public, but firm and impersonal on occasions calling for regulation and control. A police officer should understand that his primary purpose is to prevent violations, not to arrest people. He should recognize the line of demarcation between a police function and passing judgment which is a court function. On the other side, a public that cooperates with the police, that supports them in their efforts and that observes laws and regulations, may be said to have a desirable attitude.

11. In accordance with this paragraph, the PROPER attitude for a police officer to take is to   11.____

    A. be pleasant and sympathetic at all times
    B. be friendly, firm, and impartial
    C. be stern and severe in meting out justice to all
    D. avoid being rude, except in those cases where the public is uncooperative

12. Assume that an officer is assigned by his superior officer to a busy traffic intersection and is warned to be on the lookout for motorists who skip the light or who are speeding. According to this paragraph, it would be proper for the officer in this assignment to   12.____

    A. give a summons to every motorist whose ear was crossing when the light changed
    B. hide behind a truck and wait for drivers who violate traffic laws
    C. select at random motorists who seem to be impatient and lecture them sternly on traffic safety
    D. stand on post in order to deter violations and give offenders a summons or a warning as required

13. According to this paragraph, a police officer must realize that the primary purpose of police work is to   13.____

    A. provide proper police service in a courteous manner
    B. decide whether those who violate the law should be punished
    C. arrest those who violate laws
    D. establish a proper employer-employee relationship

Questions 14-15.

DIRECTIONS: Answer questions 14 and 15 SOLELY on the basis of the following paragraph.

If a motor vehicle fails to pass inspection, the owner will be given a rejection notice by the inspection station. Repairs must be made within ten days after this notice is issued. It is not necessary to have the required adjustment or repairs made at the station where the inspection occurred. The vehicle may be taken to any other garage. Re-inspection after repairs may be made at any official inspection station, not necessarily the same station which made the initial inspection. The registration of any motor vehicle for which an inspection sticker has not been obtained as required, or which is not repaired and inspected within ten days after inspection indicates defects, is subject to suspension. A vehicle cannot be used on public highways while its registration is under suspension.

14. According to the above paragraph, the owner of a car which does NOT pass inspection must

   A. have repairs made at the same station which rejected his car
   B. take the car to another station and have it re-inspected
   C. have repairs made anywhere and then have the car re-inspected
   D. not use the car on a public highway until the necessary repairs have been made

15. According to the above paragraph, the one of the following which may be cause for suspension of the registration of a vehicle is that

   A. an inspection sticker was issued before the rejection notice had been in force for ten days
   B. it was not re-inspected by the station that rejected it originally
   C. it was not re-inspected either by the station that rejected it originally or by the garage which made the repairs
   D. it has not had defective parts repaired within ten days after inspection

Questions 16-20.

DIRECTIONS: Answer questions 16 to 20 SOLELY on the basis of the following paragraph.

If we are to study crime in its widest social setting, we will find a variety of conduct which, although criminal in the legal sense, is not offensive to the moral conscience of a considerable number of persons. Traffic violations, for example, do not brand the offender as guilty of moral offense. In fact, the recipient of a traffic ticket is usually simply the subject of some good-natured joking by his friends. Although there may be indignation among certain groups of citizens against gambling and liquor law violations, these activities are often tolerated, if not openly supported, by the more numerous residents of the community. Indeed, certain social and service clubs regularly conduct gambling games and lotteries for the purpose of raising funds. Some communities regard violations involving the sale of liquor with little concern in order to profit from increased license fees and taxes paid by dealers. The thousand and one forms of political graft and corruption which infest our urban centers only occasionally arouse public condemnation and official action.

16. According to the paragraph, all types of illegal conduct are

   A. condemned by all elements of the community
   B. considered a moral offense, although some are tolerated by a few citizens
   C. violations of the law, but some are acceptable to certain elements of the community
   D. found in a social setting which is not punishable by law

17. According to the paragraph, traffic violations are generally considered by society as

   A. crimes requiring the maximum penalty set by the law
   B. more serious than violations of the liquor laws

C. offenses against the morals of the community
D. relatively minor offenses requiring minimum punishment

18. According to the paragraph, a lottery conducted for the purpose of raising funds for a church   18.____

    A. is considered a serious violation of law
    B. may be tolerated by a community which has laws against gambling
    C. may be conducted under special laws demanded by the more numerous residents of a community
    D. arouses indignation in most communities

19. On the basis of the paragraph, the MOST likely reaction in the community to a police raid on a gambling casino would be   19.____

    A. more an attitude of indifference than interest in the raid
    B. general approval of the raid
    C. condemnation of the raid by most people
    D. demand for further action since this raid is not sufficient to end gambling activities

20. The one of the following which BEST describes the central thought of this paragraph and would be MOST suitable as a title for it is   20.____

    A. CRIME AND THE POLICE
    B. PUBLIC CONDEMNATION OF GRAFT AND CORRUPTION
    C. GAMBLING IS NOT ALWAYS A VICIOUS BUSINESS
    D. PUBLIC ATTITUDE TOWARD LAW VIOLATIONS

Questions 21-23.

DIRECTIONS: Answer questions 21 to 23 SOLELY on the basis of the following paragraph.

   The law enforcement agency is one of the most important agencies in the field of juvenile delinquency prevention. This is so not because of the social work connected with this problem, however, for this is not a police matter, but because the officers are usually the first to come in contact with the delinquent. The manner of arrest and detention makes a deep impression upon him and affects his life-long attitude toward society and the law. The juvenile court is perhaps the most important agency in this work. Contrary to the general opinion, however, it is not primarily concerned with putting children into correctional schools. The main purpose of the juvenile court is to save the child and to develop his emotional make-up in order that he can grow up to be a decent and well-balanced citizen. The system of probation is the means whereby the court seeks to accomplish these goals.

21. According to this paragraph, police work is an important part of a program to prevent juvenile delinquency because   21.____

    A. social work is no longer considered important in juvenile delinquency prevention
    B. police officers are the first to have contact with the delinquent
    C. police officers jail the offender in order to be able to change his attitude toward society and the law
    D. it is the first step in placing the delinquent in jail

22. According to this paragraph, the CHIEF purpose of the juvenile court is to

    A. punish the child for his offense
    B. select a suitable correctional school for the delinquent
    C. use available means to help the delinquent become a better person
    D. provide psychiatric care for the delinquent

23. According to this paragraph, the juvenile court directs the development of delinquents under its care CHIEFLY by

    A. placing the child under probation
    B. sending the child to a correctional school
    C. keeping the delinquent in prison
    D. returning the child to his home

Questions 24-27.

DIRECTIONS: Answer questions 24 to 27 SOLELY on the basis of the following paragraph.

When a vehicle has been disabled in the tunnel, the officer on patrol in this zone shall press the EMERGENCY TRUCK light button. In the fast lane, red lights will go on throughout the tunnel; in the slow lane, amber lights will go on throughout the tunnel. The yellow zone light will go on at each signal control station throughout the tunnel and will flash the number of the zone in which the stoppage has occurred. A red flashing pilot light will appear only at the signal control station at which the EMERGENCY TRUCK button was pressed. The emergency garage will receive an audible and visual signal indicating the signal control station at which the EMERGENCY TRUCK button was pressed. The garage officer shall acknowledge receipt of the signal by pressing the acknowledgment button. This will cause the pilot light at the operated signal control station in the tunnel to cease flashing and to remain steady. It is an answer to the officer at the operated signal control station that the emergency truck is responding to the call.

24. According to this paragraph, when the EMERGENCY TRUCK light button is pressed,

    A. amber lights will go on in every lane throughout the tunnel
    B. emergency signal lights will go on only in the lane in which the disabled vehicle happens to be
    C. red lights will go on in the fast lane throughout the tunnel
    D. pilot lights at all signal control stations will turn amber

25. According to this paragraph, the number of the zone in which the stoppage has occurred is flashed

    A. immediately after all the lights in the tunnel turn red
    B. by the yellow zone light at each signal control station
    C. by the emergency truck at the point of stoppage
    D. by the emergency garage

26. According to this paragraph, an officer near the disabled vehicle will know that the emergency tow truck is coming when

    A. the pilot light at the operated signal control station appears and flashes red
    B. an audible signal is heard in the tunnel

C. the zone light at the operated signal control station turns red
D. the pilot light at the operated signal control station becomes steady

27. Under the system described in the paragraph, it would be CORRECT to come to the conclusion that

    A. officers at all signal control stations are expected to acknowledge that they have received the stoppage signal
    B. officers at all signal control stations will know where the stoppage has occurred
    C. all traffic in both lanes of that side of the tunnel in which the stoppage has occurred must stop until the emergency truck has arrived
    D. there are two emergency garages, each able to respond to stoppages in traffic going in one particular direction

Questions 28-30.

DIRECTIONS: Answer questions 28 to 30 SOLELY on the basis of the following paragraphs.

In cases of accident, it is most important for an officer to obtain the name, age, residence, occupation, and a full description of the person injured, names and addresses of witnesses. He shall also obtain a statement of the attendant circumstances. He shall carefully note contributory conditions, if any, such as broken pavement, excavation, tights not burning, snow and ice on the roadway, etc. He shall enter all facts in his memorandum book and on Form 17 or Form 18 and promptly transmit the original of the form to his superior officer and the duplicate to headquarters.

An officer shall render reasonable assistance to sick or injured persons. If the circumstances appear to require the services of a physician, he shall summon a physician by telephoning the superior officer on duty and notifying him of the apparent nature of the illness or accident and the location where the physician will be required. He may summon other officers to assist if circumstances warrant.

In case of an accident or where a person is sick on city property, an officer shall obtain the information necessary to fill out card Form 18 and record this in his memorandum book and promptly telephone the facts to his superior officer. He shall deliver the original card at the expiration of his tour to his superior officer and transmit the duplicate to headquarters.

28. According to this quotation, the MOST important consideration in any report on a case of accident or injury is to

    A. obtain all the facts
    B. telephone his superior officer at once
    C. obtain a statement of the attendant circumstances
    D. determine ownership of the property on which the accident occurred

29. According to this quotation, in the case of an accident on city property, the officer should always

    A. summon a physician before filling out any forms or making any entries in his memorandum book
    B. give his superior officer on duty a prompt report by telephone

C. immediately bring the original of Form 18 to his superior officer on duty
D. call at least one other officer to the scene to witness conditions

30. If the procedures stated in this quotation were followed for all accidents in the city, an impartial survey of accidents occurring during any period of time in this city may be MOST easily made by

    A. asking a typical officer to show you his memorandum book
    B. having a superior officer investigate whether contributory conditions mentioned by witnesses actually exist
    C. checking all the records of all superior officers
    D. checking the duplicate card files at headquarters

Questions 31-55.

DIRECTIONS: In each of questions 31 to 55, select the lettered word or phrase which means MOST NEARLY the same as the first word in the row.

31. RENDEZVOUS
    A. parade   B. neighborhood
    C. meeting place   D. wander about

32. EMINENT
    A. noted   B. rich   C. rounded   D. nearby

33. CAUSTIC
    A. cheap   B. sweet   C. evil   D. sharp

34. BARTER
    A. annoy   B. trade   C. argue   D. cheat

35. APTITUDE
    A. friendliness   B. talent
    C. conceit   D. generosity

36. PROTRUDE
    A. project   B. defend   C. choke   D. boast

37. FORTITUDE
    A. disposition   B. restlessness
    C. courage   D. poverty

38. PRELUDE
    A. introduction   B. meaning
    C. prayer   D. secret

39. SECLUSION
    A. primitive   B. influence
    C. imagination   D. privacy

40. RECTIFY
    A. correct   B. construct   C. divide   D. scold

41. TRAVERSE
    A. rotate   B. compose   C. train   D. cross

42. ALLEGE
    A. raise   B. convict   C. declare   D. chase

43. MENIAL
    A. pleasant   B. unselfish
    C. humble   D. stupid

44. DEPLETE
    A. exhaust   B. gather   C. repay   D. close

45. ERADICATE
    A. construct   B. advise   C. destroy   D. exclaim

46. CAPITULATE
    A. cover   B. surrender   C. receive   D. execute

47. RESTRAIN
    A. restore   B. drive   C. review   D. limit

48. AMALGAMATE
    A. join   B. force   C. correct   D. clash

49. DEJECTED
    A. beaten   B. speechless
    C. weak   D. low-spirited

50. DETAIN
    A. hide   B. accuse   C. hold   D. mislead

KEY (CORRECT ANSWERS)

1. A	11. B	21. B	31. C	41. D
2. C	12. D	22. C	32. A	42. C
3. B	13. A	23. A	33. D	43. C
4. C	14. C	24. C	34. B	44. A
5. D	15. D	25. B	35. B	45. C
6. A	16. C	26. D	36. A	46. B
7. B	17. D	27. B	37. C	47. D
8. A	18. B	28. A	38. A	48. A
9. A	19. A	29. B	39. D	49. D
10. C	20. D	30. D	40. A	50. C

TEST 2

DIRECTIONS: Each question or incomplete statement is followed by several suggested answers or completions. Select the one that BEST answers the question or completes the statement. *PRINT THE LETTER OF THE CORRECT ANSWER IN THE SPACE AT THE RIGHT.*

1. AMPLE 1.____
   A. necessary   B. plentiful   C. protected   D. tasty

2. EXPEDITE 2.____
   A. sue   B. omit   C. hasten   D. verify

3. FRAGMENT 3.____
   A. simple tool   B. broken part
   C. basic outline   D. weakness

4. ADVERSARY 4.____
   A. thief   B. partner   C. loser   D. foe

5. ACHIEVE 5.____
   A. accomplish   B. begin   C. develop   D. urge

Questions 6-10.

DIRECTIONS: Answer Questions 6 to 10 on the basis of the information given in the table on the following page. The numbers which have been omitted from the table can be calculated from the other numbers which are given.

NUMBER OF DWELLING UNITS CONSTRUCTED

Year	Private one-family houses	In private apt. houses	In public housing	Total dwelling units
1996	4,500	500	600	5,600
1997	9,200	5,300	2,800	17,300
1998	8,900	12,800	6,800	28,500
1999	12,100	15,500	7,100	34,700
2000	?	12,200	14,100	39,200
2001	10,200	26,000	8,600	44,800
2002	10,300	17,900	7,400	35,600
2003	11,800	18,900	7,700	38,400
2004	12,700	22,100	8,400	43,200
2005	13,300	24,300	8,100	45,700
TOTALS	105,900	?	?	?

6. According to this table, the average number of public housing units constructed yearly during the period 1996 through 2005 was 6.____

   A. 7,160   B. 6,180   C. 7,610   D. 6,810

43

7. Of the following, the two years in which the number of private one-family homes constructed was GREATEST for the two years together is

   A. 1998 and 1999
   B. 1997 and 2003
   C. 1998 and 2004
   D. 2001 and 2002

8. For the entire period of 1996 through 2005, the total of all private one-family houses constructed exceeded the total of all public housing units constructed by

   A. 34,300   B. 45,700   C. 50,000   D. 83,900

9. Of the total number of private apartment house dwelling units constructed in the ten years given in the table, the percentage which was constructed in 2002 was MOST NEARLY

   A. 5%   B. 11%   C. 16%   D. 21%

10. Considering dwelling units of all types, the average number constructed annually in the period from 2001 through 2005 was GREATER than the average number constructed annually in the period from 1996 through 2000 by

    A. 16,480   B. 33,320   C. 79,300   D. 82,400

11. A car speeds through the toll entrance of a 2 1/4 mile long bridge without paying the toll and reaches the other end of the bridge 1 minute and 30 seconds later. The car was traveling MOST NEARLY at a rate of _____ miles per hour.

    A. 60   B. 70   C. 80   D. 90

12. During one week, 21,500 vehicles passed through the toll booths of a certain bridge. Of these, 550 were buses, 2,230 were trucks, and the rest were passenger cars. The toll charges were $3.50 for a passenger car, $7 for a truck and $14 for a bus. The total income for the week was

    A. $80,850   B. $88,830   C. $102,550   D. $109,550

13. A bullet fired from a revolver travels 100 feet the first second, and each succeeding second it travels a distance 10% less than during the immediately preceding second. The number of feet the bullet will have traveled at the end of the fourth second is MOST NEARLY

    A. 272   B. 320   C. 344   D. 360

14. An officer receives a uniform allowance of $500 a year in a lump sum. Of this amount, he spends $180 for a winter jacket and 40% of the remainder for two pairs of trousers. The officer now wishes to buy a winter overcoat which costs $240.
    The percentage of the purchase price of the overcoat by which he will be short is

    A. 20%   B. 25%   C. 48%   D. 60%

15. It has been suggested that small light cars can be used for certain kinds of police work. These light vehicles can run 30 miles per gallon of gasoline as contrasted with standard cars which run only 15 miles per gallon. Assume gasoline costs the city $3.75 per gallon. During 9,000 miles of travel, use of the small light car in preference to the standard car would result in a saving in gasoline costs of MOST NEARLY

    A. $1,125   B. $1,500   C. $1,875   D. $2,250

16. Out of a total of 34,750 felony complaints in 2006, 14,200 involved burglary. In 2005, there was a total of 32,300 felony complaints of which 12,800 were burglary.
Of the increase in felonies from 2005 to 2006, the increase in burglaries comprised APPROXIMATELY

    A. 27%   B. 37%   C. 47%   D. 57%

17. A certain city department has two offices which issue permits, one office handling twice as many applicants as the other. The smaller office grants permits to 40% of its applicants. The larger office handling twice as many applicants grants permits to 60% of its applicants.
If there were 900 applicants at both offices together on a given day, the total number of permits granted by both offices would be MOST NEARLY

    A. 420   B. 450   C. 480   D. 510

18. If a co-worker is not breathing after receiving an electric shock but is no longer in contact with the electricity, it is MOST important for you to

    A. avoid moving him
    B. wrap the victim in a blanket
    C. start artificial respiration promptly
    D. force him to take hot liquids

19. Employees using supplies from one of the first-aid kits available throughout the building are required to submit an immediate report of the occurrence.
Logical reasoning shows that the MOST important reason for this report is so that the

    A. supplies used will be sure to be replaced
    B. first-aid kit can be properly sealed again
    C. employee will be credited for his action
    D. record of first-aid supplies will be up-to-date

20. The BEST IMMEDIATE first-aid treatment for a scraped knee is to

    A. apply plain vaseline   B. wash it with soap and water
    C. apply heat   D. use a knee splint

21. Artificial respiration after a severe electrical shock is ALWAYS necessary when the shock results in

    A. unconsciousness   B. stoppage of breathing
    C. bleeding   D. a burn

22. The authority gives some of its maintenance employees instruction in first aid.
The MOST likely reason for doing this is to

    A. eliminate the need for calling a doctor in case of accident
    B. provide temporary emergency treatment in case of accident
    C. lower the cost of accidents to the authority
    D. reduce the number of accidents

23. The BEST IMMEDIATE first aid if a chemical solution splashes into the eyes is to

    A. protect the eyes from the light by bandaging
    B. rub the eyes dry with a towel

C. cause tears to flow by staring at a bright light
D. flush the eyes with large quantities of clean water

24. If you had to telephone for an ambulance because of an accident, the MOST important information for you to give the person who answered the telephone would be the

A. exact time of the accident
B. cause of the accident
C. place where the ambulance is needed
D. names and addresses of those injured

25. If a person has a deep puncture wound in his finger caused by a sharp nail, the BEST IMMEDIATE first aid procedure would be to

A. encourage bleeding by exerting pressure around the injured area
B. stop all bleeding
C. prevent air from reaching the wound
D. probe the wound for steel particles

26. In addition to cases of submersion, artificial respiration is a recommended first aid procedure for

A. sunstroke   B. electrical shock   C. chemical poisoning   D. apoplexy

27. Assume that you are called on to render first aid to a man injured in an accident. You find he is bleeding profusely, is unconscious, and has a broken arm. There is a strong odor of alcohol about him.
The FIRST thing for which you should treat him is the

A. bleeding   B. unconsciousness   C. broken arm   D. alcoholism

28. In applying first aid for removal of a foreign body in the eye, an important precaution to be observed is NOT to

A. attempt to wash out the foreign body
B. bring the upper eyelid down over the lower
C. rub the eye
D. touch or attempt to remove a speck on the lower lid

29. The one of the following symptoms which is LEAST likely to indicate that a person involved in an accident requires first aid for shock is that

A. he has fainted twice
B. his face is red and flushed
C. his skin is wet with sweat
D. his pulse is rapid

30. When giving first aid to a person suffering from shock as a result of an auto accident, it is MOST important to

A. massage him in order to aid blood circulation
B. have him sip whiskey
C. prop him up in a sitting position
D. cover the person and keep him warm

Questions 31-34.

DIRECTIONS: Answer questions 31 to 34 SOLELY on the basis of the following paragraph.

Assume that you are an officer assigned to one large office which issues and receives applications for various permits and licenses. The office consists of one section where the necessary forms are issued; another section where fees are paid to a cashier; and desks where applicants are interviewed and their forms reviewed and completed. There is also a section containing tables and chairs where persons may sit and fill out their applications before being interviewed or paying the fees. your duties consist of answering simple questions, directing the public to the correct section of the office, and maintaining order.

31. A man who speaks English poorly asks you for assistance in obtaining and filling out an application for a permit. You should 31.____

    A. send him to an interviewer who can assist him
    B. try to determine what permit he wants and fill out the form for him
    C. refer the man to the office supervisor
    D. ask another applicant to help this person

32. The office becomes noisy and crowded, with people milling around waiting for service at the various sections. 32.____
Of the following, the BEST action for you to take is to

    A. stand in a prominent place and in a loud voice request the people to be quiet
    B. direct all the people not being served to wait at the unoccupied tables until you call them
    C. line up the people in front of each section and keep the lines in good order
    D. tell the people to form a single line outside the office and let in a few at a time

33. A man who has just been denied a permit becomes angry and shouts that if he "knew the right people" he too could get a permit. His behavior is disturbing the office. 33.____
Of the following, the BEST action for you to take is to

    A. order the man to leave at once since his business is done
    B. tell the man to be quiet and file another application
    C. suggest to the supervisor that a pamphlet be prepared explaining the requirements for permits in simple language
    D. ask an interviewer to explain the requirements for his permit to the person and his right of appeal

34. Just before the close of business, a man rushes in and insists on being interviewed for a permit because his present one expires that night. 34.____
Of the following, the BEST action for you to take is to

    A. tell the man that the office is closed
    B. tell the man that there will be no penalty if he returns early the next morning
    C. inquire if an interviewer is still available to take care of him and send him to that desk
    D. tell the cashier to collect the fee and tell the man to return the next morning for an interview

35. Fingerprints are often taken of applicants for licenses. Of the following, the MOST valid reason for this procedure is that

    A. the license of someone who commits a crime can be more readily revoked
    B. applicants can be checked for possible criminal records
    C. it helps to make sure that the proper license fee is paid
    D. a complete employment record of the applicant is obtained

36. Assume that an officer is on patrol at 2 A.M. He notices that the night light inside one of the stores in a public building is out. The store is locked.
    Of the following, the FIRST action for him to take at this time is to

    A. continue on his patrol since the light probably burned out
    B. enter the store by any means possible so he can check it
    C. report the matter to his superior
    D. shine his flashlight through the window to look for anything unusual

37. In questioning a man suspected of having committed a theft, the BEST procedure for an officer to follow is to

    A. induce the man to express his feelings about the police, the courts, and his home environment
    B. threaten him with beatings when he refuses to answer your questions
    C. make any promises necessary to get him to confess
    D. remain calm and objective

38. As an officer, you are on duty in one of the offices of a large public building. A woman who has just finished her business with this office comes to you and reports that her son who was with her is missing.
    The one of the following which is the BEST action for you to take FIRST is to

    A. tell the mother that the child is probably all right and ask her to go to the local police station for help in finding the boy
    B. suggest that the mother wait in the office until the child turns up
    C. check nearby offices in an attempt to locate the child
    D. telephone the local police station and ask if any reports fitting the description of the child have been received

39. An officer assigned to patrol inside a public building at night has observed two men standing outside the doorway. Of the following, the MOST appropriate action for the officer to take FIRST is to

    A. approach the two men and ask them why they are standing there
    B. hide and wait for the two men to take some action
    C. phone the local police station and ask for help since these men may be planning criminal action
    D. check all the entrance doors of the building to make sure that they are locked

40. It is standard practice for special officers to inspect the restrooms in public buildings. This is done at regular intervals while on patrol.
    Of the following, the BEST reason for this practice is to

    A. inspect sanitary conditions
    B. discourage loiterers and potential criminals

C. check the ventilation
D. determine if all the equipment and plumbing is working properly

41. While on duty in the evening as an officer assigned to a public building, you receive a report that a card game is going on in one of the offices. Gambling is forbidden on government property.
Of the following, the BEST course of action for you to take is to

   A. go to the office and order the card players to leave
   B. ignore the complaint since this is probably just harmless social card playing
   C. report the matter to the building manager the next day
   D. go to the office and, if warranted, issue an appropriate warning

42. It has been suggested that special officers establish good working relationships with the local police officers of the police department on duty in the neighborhood.
Of the following, the MOST valid reason for this practice is that

   A. a spirit of good feeling and high morale will be created among members of the police department
   B. local police officers will probably cooperate more readily with the special officer
   C. local police officers can take over the building patrol duties of the special officer in case he is absent
   D. special officers have an even stronger obligation than ordinary citizens to cooperate with the police

43. It has been proposed that an officer assigned to a public building at night remain at one location in the building, instead of walking on patrol through the building.
This proposal is

   A. *bad;* chiefly because the officer would probably sit instead of stand at the proper location
   B. *good;* chiefly because the officer could do a better job of watching the entire building from one point
   C. *bad;* chiefly because anyone seeking to enter the building for illegal purposes might be able to do so at a point other than where the special officer is on duty
   D. *good;* chiefly because his supervisors would know exactly where to find him

44. In a busy office, an officer has been assigned the duty of making sure that the public is served in the order of their arrival at the office and that some employee is always taking care of a person desiring help.
Of the following, the BEST method for the officer to follow is to

   A. line up the persons in the waiting room
   B. give a numbered ticket to each person waiting and call out the numbers, in order, when an employee becomes available
   C. loudly announce "next" when an employee is available to serve someone
   D. seat one person next to each employee's desk and let the others wait for the first vacant seat

45. Two men have broken into and entered a building at night. The officer on duty at this building sees them, chases them out, and then observes them in the adjoining building.
Of the following, the BEST course of action for the officer to take is to

   A. notify the local police station and be ready to aid the police
   B. enter the adjoining building to find the men
   C. notify the manager of his own building
   D. continue on duty since these men have left the building for which he is responsible

46. While an officer is on duty in a crowded waiting room, he finds a woman's purse on the floor.
Of the following, the FIRST course of action for him to take is to

   A. hold it up in the air, ask who owns it, and give it to whoever claims it
   B. keep the purse until someone claims it
   C. immediately deliver the purse to the "lost and found" desk
   D. ask the lady who is nearest to him if she lost a purse

47. Special officers often have the power of arrest.
Of the following, the BEST reason for this practice is to

   A. have the officer always arrest any person who refuses to obey his orders
   B. aid in maintaining order in places where he is assigned
   C. promote good public relations
   D. aid in preventing illegal use of public buildings by tenants or employees

48. An officer has told a mother that he found her son writing on the walls of the building with chalk. The mother tells the officer that he should be more concerned with "crooks" than with children's minor pranks.
Of the following, the BEST answer for the officer to make to this woman is that

   A. children should be taught good conduct by their parents
   B. damage to public property means higher taxes
   C. serious criminals often begin their careers with minor violations
   D. it is his duty to enforce all rules and regulations

49. A man asks you, a special officer, where to get a certain kind of license not issued in your office. You don't know where such licenses are issued.
Of the following, the BEST procedure for you to follow is to

   A. refer him to the manager of the office
   B. get the information if you can and give it to the man
   C. tell the man to inquire at any police station house
   D. tell the man that you just do not know

50. Special officers are not permitted to ask private citizens to buy tickets for dances or other such social functions, not even when such functions are operated by charitable organizations. Of the following, the BEST reason for this rule is that

   A. private citizens are under no obligation to buy any such tickets
   B. not all groups are allowed equal opportunity in the sale of their tickets
   C. private citizens might complain to officials
   D. private citizens might feel they would not get proper service unless they bought such tickets

KEY (CORRECT ANSWERS)

1. B	11. D	21. B	31. A	41. D
2. C	12. B	22. B	32. C	42. B
3. B	13. C	23. D	33. D	43. C
4. D	14. A	24. C	34. C	44. B
5. A	15. A	25. A	35. B	45. A
6. A	16. D	26. B	36. D	46. C
7. C	17. C	27. A	37. D	47. B
8. A	18. C	28. C	38. C	48. D
9. B	19. A	29. B	39. D	49. B
10. A	20. B	30. D	40. B	50. D

SOLUTIONS TO ARITHMETIC PROBLEMS

11. $2\frac{1}{4}$ miles are completed in 1 1/2 minutes (1 minute and 30 seconds)

    $\therefore 2\frac{1}{4} \div 1\frac{1}{2}$ = rate per minute

    $= \frac{9}{4} \div 1\frac{1}{2}$

    $= \frac{9}{4} \div \frac{3}{2}$

    $= \frac{9}{4} \times \frac{2}{3}$

    $= \frac{3}{2}$ miles per minute

    $\therefore \frac{3}{2} \times 60$ (minutes in an hour) = rate per hour = 90 miles per hour

    (Ans. D)

12. 550 + 2230 = 2780; 21,500 - 2780 = 18,720 passengers

550 buses at $14.00	=	$ 7,700
2230 trucks at $7.00	=	15,610
18720 passengers at $3.50	=	65,520
		$88,830

    (Ans. B)

13. Given: speed = 100 feet the first second

100 - 10 (10% of 100)	=	90 feet - the second second
90 - 9 (10% of 90)	=	81 feet - the third second
81 - 8.1 (10% of 81)	=	72.9 feet - the fourth second
		343.9 (total at end of the fourth second)

    (Ans. C)

14. Given: 500 = uniform allowance

$500 - 180	=	$320	(amount left after buying winter jacket)
$320 x 40%	=	$128	(amount spent for two pairs of trousers)
$320 - 128	=	$192	(amount now left)

    Since the winter overcoat costs $240, he is now short $48 ($240 - 192) or 20% of the purchase price of the overcoat. (48/240 = $\frac{1}{5}$ = 20%)

(Ans. A)

15. Light care: 9000(miles)÷30(miles per gallon)×3.75(per gallon)

$$= \frac{9000}{30} \times 3.75$$
$$= 300 \times 3.75$$
$$= \$1,125 \text{ (total gasoline cost)}$$

Standard cars: 9000 (miles) ÷ 15 (miles per gallon) x 3.75

$$= \frac{9000}{15} \times 3.75$$
$$= 600 \times 3.75$$
$$= \$2,250 \text{ (total gasoline cost)}$$

∴ use of light car would result in a saving in gasoline costs of $1,125 ($2,250 - $1,125).

(Ans. A)

16.
2006:	14,200	(burglary)
2005:	12,800	(burglary)
	1,400	(increase in burglaries)
2006:	34,750	(felony)
2005:	32,300	(felony)
	2,450	(increase in felonies

$$\therefore 1400 \div 2450 = \frac{1400}{2450} = .57$$

WORK

```
        .57
2450)1400.0
     1225.0
      175.00
      171.50
```

(Ans. D)

17. Given: smaller office: grants permits to 40% of 1/3 of the total number of applicants (900)

larger office: grants permits to 60% of 2/3 of the total number of applicants (900)

Solving: smaller office: $.40 \times \frac{1}{3} \times 900 = 120$ permits

larger office: $.60 \times \frac{2}{3} \times 900 = 360$ permits
                                              480 permits (total)

(Ans. C)

EXAMINATION SECTION
TEST 1

DIRECTIONS: Each question or incomplete statement is followed by several suggested answers or completions. Select the one that BEST answers the question or completes the statement. *PRINT THE LETTER OF THE CORRECT ANSWER IN THE SPACE AT THE RIGHT.*

1. Of the following, the MOST important single factor in any building security program is 1.____

   A. a fool-proof employee identification system
   B. an effective control of entrances and exits
   C. bright illumination of all outside areas
   D. clearly marking public and non-public areas

2. There is general agreement that the BEST criterion of what is a good physical security system in a large public building is 2.____

   A. the number of uniformed officers needed to patrol sensitive areas
   B. how successfully the system prevents rather than detects violations
   C. the number of persons caught in the act of committing criminal offenses
   D. how successfully the system succeeds in maintaining good public relations

3. Which one of the following statements most correctly expresses the CHIEF reason why women were originally made eligible for appointment to the position of officer? 3.____

   A. Certain tasks in security protection can be performed best by assigning women.
   B. More women than men are available to fill many vacancies in this position.
   C. The government wants more women in law enforcement because of their better attendance records.
   D. Women can no longer be barred from any government jobs because of sex.

4. The MOST BASIC purpose of patrol by officers is to 4.____

   A. eliminate as much as possible the opportunity for successful misconduct
   B. investigate criminal complaints and accident cases
   C. give prompt assistance to employees and citizens in distress or requesting their help
   D. take persons into custody who commit criminal offenses against persons and property

5. The highest quality of patrol service is MOST generally obtained by 5.____

   A. frequently changing the post assignments of each officer
   B. assigning officers to posts of equal size
   C. assigning problem officers to the least desirable posts
   D. assigning the same officers to the same posts

6. The one of the following requirements which is MOST essential to the successful performance of patrol duty by individual officers is their 6.____

   A. ability to communicate effectively with higher-level officers
   B. prompt signalling according to a prescribed schedule to insure post coverages at all times

55

C. knowledge of post conditions and post hazards
D. willingness to cover large areas during periods of critical manpower shortages

7. Officers on patrol are constantly warned to be on the alert for suspicious persons, actions, and circumstances.
With this in mind, a senior officer should emphasize the need for them to

A. be cautious and suspicious when dealing officially with any civilian regardless of the latter's overt actions or the circumstances surrounding his dealings with the police
B. keep looking for the unusual persons, actions, and circumstances on their posts and pay less attention to the usual
C. take aggressive police action immediately against any unusual person or condition detected on their posts, regardless of any other circumstances
D. become thoroughly familiar with the usual on their posts so as to be better able to detect the unusual

8. Of primary importance in the safeguarding of property from theft is a good central lock and key issuance and control system.
Which one of the following recommendations about maintaining such a control system would be LEAST acceptable?

A. In selecting locks to be used for the various gates, building, and storage areas, consideration should be given to the amount of security desired.
B. Master keys should have no markings that will identify them as such and the list of holders of these keys should be frequently reviewed to determine the continuing necessity for the individuals having them.
C. Whenever keys for outside doors or gates or for other doors which permit access to important buildings and areas are misplaced, the locks should be immediately changed or replaced pending an investigation.
D. Whenever an employee fails to return a borrowed key at the time specified, a prompt investigation should be made by the security force.

9. In a crowded building, a fire develops in the basement, and smoke enters the crowded rooms on the first floor. Of the following, the BEST action for an officer to take after an alarm is turned in is to

A. call out a warning that the building is on fire and that everyone should evacuate because of the immediate danger
B. call all of the officers together for an emergency meeting and discuss a plan of action
C. immediately call for assistance from the local police station to help in evacuating the crowd
D. tell everyone that there is a fire in the building next door and that they should move out onto the streets through available exits

10. Which of the following is in a key position to carry out successfully a safety program of an agency? The

A. building engineer   B. bureau chiefs
C. immediate supervisors   D. public relations director

11. It is GENERALLY considered that a daily roll call inspection, which checks to see that the officers and their equipment are in good order, is

    A. *desirable,* chiefly because it informs the superior officer what men will have to purchase new uniforms within a month
    B. *desirable,* chiefly because the public forms their impressions of the organization from the appearance of the officers
    C. *undesirable,* chiefly because this kind of daily inspection unnecessarily delays officers in getting to their assigned patrol posts
    D. *undesirable,* chiefly because roll call inspection usually misses individuals reporting to work late

12. A supervising officer in giving instructions to a group of officers on the principles of accident investigation remarked, "A conclusion that appears reasonable will often be changed by exploring a factor of apparently little importance".
    Which one of the following precautions does this statement emphasize as MOST important in any accident investigation?

    A. Every accident clue should be fully investigated.
    B. Accidents should not be too promptly investigated.
    C. Only specially trained officers should investigate accidents.
    D. Conclusions about accident causes are highly unreliable.

13. On a rainy day, a senior officer found that 9 of his 50 officers reported to work. What percentage of his officers was ABSENT?

    A. 18%   B. 80%   C. 82%   D. 90%

14. Officer A and Officer B work at the same post on the same days, but their hours are different. Officer A comes to work at 9:00 A.M. and leaves at 5:00 P.M., with a lunch period between 12:15 P.M. and 1:15 P.M. Officer B comes to work at 10:50 A.M. and works until 6:50 P.M., and he takes an hour for lunch between 3:00 P.M. and 4:00 P.M. What is the total amount of time between 9:00 A.M. and 6:50 P.M. that only ONE officer will be on duty?

    A. 4 hours   B. 4 hours and 40 minutes
    C. 5 hours   D. 5 hours and 40 minutes

15. An officer's log recorded the following attendance of 30 officers:

    | Monday | 20 | present; | 10 | absent |
    | Tuesday | 28 | present; | 2 | absent |
    | Wednesday | 30 | present; | 0 | absent |
    | Thursday | 21 | present; | 9 | absent |
    | Friday | 16 | present; | 14 | absent |
    | Saturday | 11 | present; | 19 | absent |
    | Sunday | 14 | present; | 16 | absent |

    On the average, how many men were present on the weekdays (Monday - Friday)?

    A. 21   B. 23   C. 25   D. 27

16. An angry woman is being questioned by an officer when she begins shouting abuses at him.
   The BEST of the following procedures for the officer to follow is to

   A. leave the room until she has cooled off
   B. politely ignore anything she says
   C. place her under arrest by handcuffing her to a fixed object
   D. warn her that he will have to use force to restrain her making remarks

17. Of the following, which is NOT a recommended practice for an officer placing a woman offender under arrest?

   A. Assume that the offender is an innocent and virtuous person and treat her accordingly.
   B. Protect himself from attack by the woman.
   C. Refrain from using excessive physical force on the offender.
   D. Make the public aware that he is not abusing the woman.

Questions 18-21.

DIRECTIONS: Questions 18 through 21 are to be answered SOLELY on the basis of the following passage.

Specific measures for prevention of pilferage will be based on careful analysis of the conditions at each agency. The most practical and effective method to control casual pilferage is the establishment of psychological deterrents.

One of the most common means of discouraging casual pilferage is to search individuals leaving the agency at unannounced times and places. These spot searches may occasionally detect attempts at theft but greater value is realized by bringing to the attention of individuals the fact that they may be apprehended if they do attempt the illegal removal of property.

An aggressive security education program is an effective means of convincing employees that they have much more to lose than they do to gain by engaging in acts of theft. It is important for all employees to realize that pilferage is morally wrong no matter how insignificant the value of the item which is taken. In establishing any deterrent to casual pilferage, security officers must not lose sight of the fact that most employees are honest and disapprove of thievery. Mutual respect between security personnel and other employees of the agency must be maintained if the facility is to be protected from other more dangerous forms of human hazards. Any security measure which infringes on the human rights or dignity of others will jeopardize, rather than enhance, the overall protection of the agency.

18. The $100,000 yearly inventory of an agency revealed that $50 worth of goods had been stolen; the only individuals with access to the stolen materials were the employees. Of the following measures, which would the author of the preceding paragraph MOST likely recommend to a security officer?

   A. Conduct an intensive investigation of all employees to find the culprit.
   B. Make a record of the theft, but take no investigative or disciplinary action against any employee.
   C. Place a tight security check on all future movements of personnel.
   D. Remove the remainder of the material to an area with much greater security.

19. What does the passage imply is the percentage of employees whom a security officer should expect to be honest? 19._____

   A. No employee can be expected to be honest all of the time
   B. Just 50%
   C. Less than 50%
   D. More than 50%

20. According to the passage, the security officer would use which of the following methods to minimize theft in buildings with many exits when his staff is very small? 20._____

   A. Conduct an inventory of all material and place a guard near that which is most likely to be pilfered.
   B. Inform employees of the consequences of legal prosecution for pilfering.
   C. Close off the unimportant exits and have all his men concentrate on a few exits.
   D. Place a guard at each exit and conduct a casual search of individuals leaving the premises.

21. Of the following, the title BEST suited for this passage is: 21._____

   A. Control Measures for Casual Pilfering
   B. Detecting the Potential Pilferer
   C. Financial losses Resulting from Pilfering
   D. The Use of Moral Persuasion in Physical Security

22. Of the following first aid procedures, which will cause the GREATEST harm in treating a fracture? 22._____

   A. Control hemorrhages by applying direct pressure
   B. Keep the broken portion from moving about
   C. Reset a protruding bone by pressing it back into place
   D. Treat the suffering person for shock

23. During a snowstorm, a man comes to you complaining of frostbitten hands. PROPER first aid treatment in this case is to 23._____

   A. place the hands under hot running water
   B. place the hands in lukewarm water
   C. call a hospital and wait for medical aid
   D. rub the hands in melting snow

24. While on duty, an officer sees a woman apparently in a state of shock. Of the following, which one is NOT a symptom of shock? 24._____

   A. Eyes lacking luster
   B. A cold, moist forehead
   C. A shallow, irregular breathing
   D. A strong, throbbing pulse

25. You notice a man entering your building who begins coughing violently, has shortness of breath, and complains of severe chest pains. 25._____
   These symptoms are GENERALLY indicative of

   A. a heart attack   B. a stroke
   C. internal bleeding   D. an epileptic seizure

26. When an officer is required to record the rolled fingerprint impressions of a prisoner on the standard fingerprint form, the technique recommended by the F.B.I. as MOST likely to result in obtaining clear impressions is to roll

    A. all fingers away from the center of the prisoner's body
    B. all fingers toward the center of the prisoner's body
    C. the thumbs away from and the other fingers toward the center of the prisoner's body
    D. the thumbs toward and the other fingers away from the center of the prisoner's body

26._____

27. The principle which underlies the operation and use of a lie detector machine is that

    A. a person who is not telling the truth will be able to give a consistent story
    B. a guilty mind will unconsciously associate ideas in a very indicative manner
    C. the presence of emotional stress in a person will result in certain abnormal physical reactions
    D. many individuals are not afraid to lie

27._____

Questions 28-32.

DIRECTIONS: Questions 28 through 32 are based SOLELY on the following diagram and the paragraph preceding this group of questions. The paragraph will be divided into two statements. Statement one (1) consists of information given to the senior officer by an agency director; *this information will detail the specific security objectives the senior officer has to meet.* Statement two (2) gives the resources available to the senior officer.

NOTE: The questions are correctly answered only when all of the agency's objectives have been met and when the officer has used all his resources efficiently (i.e., to their maximum effectiveness) in meeting these objectives. All X's in the diagram indicate possible locations of officers' posts. Each X has a corresponding number which is to be used when referring to that location.

7 (#1)

DIAGRAM

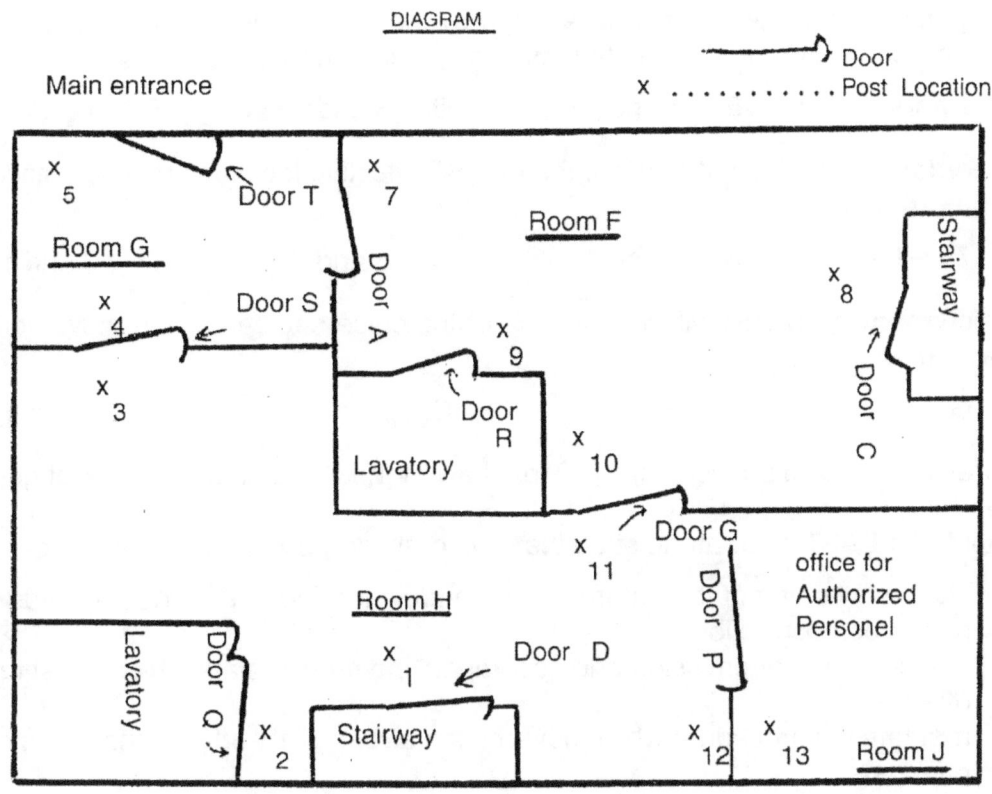

PARAGRAPH

PARAGRAPH

STATEMENT 1: Room G will be the public intake room from which persons will be directed to Room F or Room H; under no circumstances are they to enter the wrong room, and they are not to move from Room F to Room H or vice-versa. A minimum of two officers must be in each room frequented by the public at all times, and they are to keep unauthorized individuals from going to the second floor or into restricted areas. All usable entrances or exits must be covered.

STATEMENT 2: The senior officer can lock any door except the main entrance and stairway doors. He has a staff of five officers to carry out these operations.

NOTE: The senior officer is available for guard duty. Room J is an active office.

28. According to the instructions, how many officers should be assigned inside the office for authorized personnel (Room J)?

   A. 0   B. 1   C. 2   D. 3

29. In order to keep the public from moving between Room F and Room H, which door(s) can be locked without interfering with normal office operations? Door

   A. G   B. P   C. R and Q   D. S

30. When placing officers in Room H, the only way the senior officer can satisfy the agency's objectives and his manpower limitations is by placing men at locations

    A. 1 and 3   B. 1 and 12   C. 3 and 11   D. 11 and 12

31. In accordance with the instructions, the LEAST effective locations to place officers in Room F are locations

    A. 7 and 9   B. 7 and 10   C. 8 and 9   D. 9 and 10

32. In which room is it MOST difficult for each of the officers to see all the movements of the public? Room

    A. G   B. F   C. H   D. J

33. According to its own provisions, the Penal Law of the State has a number of general purposes.
    It would be LEAST accurate to state that one of these general purposes is to

    A. give fair warning of the nature of the conduct forbidden and the penalties authorized upon conviction
    B. define the act or omission and accompanying mental state which constitute each offense
    C. regulate the procedure which governs the arrest, trial and punishment of convicted offenders
    D. insure the public safety by preventing the commission of offenses through the deterrent influence of the sentences authorized upon conviction

34. Officers must be well-informed about the meaning of certain terms in connection with their enforcement duties. Which one of the following statements about such terms would be MOST accurate according to the Penal Law of the State? A(n)

    A. offense is always a crime
    B. offense is always a violation
    C. violation is never a crime
    D. felony is never an offense

35. According to the Penal Law of the State, the one of the following elements which must ALWAYS be present in order to justify the arrest of a person for criminal assault is

    A. the infliction of an actual physical injury
    B. an intent to cause an injury
    C. a threat to inflict a physical injury
    D. the use of some kind of weapon

36. A recent law of the State defines who are police officers and who are peace officers. The official title of this law is: The

    A. Criminal Code of Procedure
    B. Law of Criminal Procedure
    C. Criminal Procedure Law
    D. Code of Criminal Procedure

37. If you are required to appear in court to testify as the complainant in a criminal action, it would be MOST important for you to

    A. confine your answers to the questions asked when you are testifying
    B. help the prosecutor even if some exaggeration in your testimony may be necessary
    C. be as fair as possible to the defendant even if some details have to be omitted from your testimony
    D. avoid contradicting other witnesses testifying against the defendant

37.____

38. A senior officer is asked by the television news media to explain to the public what happened on his post during an important incident.
    When speaking with departmental permission in front of the tape recorders and cameras, the senior officer can give the MOST favorable impression of himself and his department by

    A. refusing to answer any questions but remaining calm in front of the cameras
    B. giving a detailed report of the wrong decisions made by his agency for handling the particular incident
    C. presenting the appropriate factual information in a competent way
    D. telling what should have been done during the incident and how such incidents will be handled in the future

38.____

39. Of the following suggested guidelines for officers, the one which is LEAST likely to be effective in promoting good manners and courtesy in their daily contacts with the public is:

    A. Treat inquiries by telephone in the same manner as those made in person
    B. Never look into the face of the person to whom you are speaking
    C. Never give misinformation in answer to any inquiry on a matter on which you are uncertain of the facts
    D. Show respect and consideration in both trivial and important contacts with the public

39.____

40. Assume you are an officer who has had a record of submitting late weekly reports and that you are given an order by your supervisor which is addressed to all line officers. The order states that weekly reports will be replaced by twice-weekly reports.
    The MOST logical conclusion for you to make, of the following, is:

    A. Fully detailed information was missing from your past reports
    B. Most officers have submitted late reports
    C. The supervisor needs more timely information
    D. The supervisor is attempting to punish you for your past late reports

40.____

41. A young man with long hair and "mod" clothing makes a complaint to an officer about the rudeness of another officer.
    If the senior officer is not on the premises, the officer receiving the complaint should

    A. consult with the officer who is being accused to see if the youth's story is true
    B. refer the young man to central headquarters
    C. record the complaint made against his fellow officer and ask the youth to wait until he can locate the senior officer
    D. search for the senior officer and bring him back to the site of the complainant

41.____

42. During a demonstration, which area should ALWAYS be kept clear of demonstrators?

    A. Water fountains B. Seating areas
    C. Doorways D. Restrooms

43. During demonstrations, an officer's MOST important duty is to

    A. aid the agency's employees to perform their duties
    B. promptly arrest those who might cause incidents
    C. promptly disperse the crowds of demonstrators
    D. keep the demonstrators from disrupting order

44. Of the following, what is the FIRST action a senior officer should take if a demonstration develops in his area without advance warning?

    A. Call for additional assistance from the police department
    B. Find the leaders of the demonstrators and discuss their demands
    C. See if the demonstrators intend to break the law
    D. Inform his superiors of the event taking place

45. If a senior officer is informed in the morning that a demonstration will take place during the afternoon at his assigned location, he should assemble his officers to discuss the nature and aspects of this demonstration. Of the following, the subject which it is LEAST important to discuss during this meeting is

    A. making a good impression if an officer is called before the television cameras for a personal interview
    B. the known facts and causes of the demonstration
    C. the attitude and expected behavior of the demonstrators
    D. the individual responsibilities of the officers during the demonstration

46. A male officer has probable reason to believe that a group of women occupying the ladies' toilet are using illicit drugs.
    The BEST action, of the following, for the officer to take is to

    A. call for assistance and, with the aid of such assistance, enter the toilet and escort the occupants outside
    B. ignore the situation but recommend that the ladies' toilet be closed temporarily
    C. immediately rush into the ladies' toilet and search the occupants therein
    D. knock on the door of the ladies' toilet and ask their permission to enter so that he will not be accused of trying to molest them

47. Assume that you know that a group of demonstrators will not cooperate with your request to throw handbills in a waste basket instead of on the sidewalk. You ask one of the leaders of the group, who agrees with you, to speak to the demonstrators and ask for their cooperation in this matter.
    Your request of the group leader is

    A. *desirable,* chiefly because an officer needs civilians to control the public since the officer is usually unfriendly to the views of public groups
    B. *undesirable,* chiefly because an officer should never request a civilian to perform his duties
    C. *desirable,* chiefly because the appeal of an acknowledged leader helps in gaining group cooperation

D. *undesirable,* chiefly because an institutional leader is motivated to maneuver a situation to gain his own personal advantage

48. A vague letter received from a female employee in the agency accuses an officer of improper conduct.
The initial investigative interview by the senior officer assigned to check the accusation should GENERALLY be with the

   A. accused officer
   B. female employee
   C. highest superior about disciplinary action against the officer
   D. immediate supervisor of the female employee

48._____

Questions 49-50.

DIRECTIONS: Questions 49 and 50 are to be answered SOLELY on the basis of the information in the following paragraph.

The personal conduct of each member of the Department is the primary factor in promoting desirable police-community relations. Tact, patience, and courtesy shall be strictly observed under all circumstances. A favorable public attitude toward the police must be earned; it is influenced by the personal conduct and attitude of each member of the force, by his personal integrity and courteous manner, by his respect for due process of law, by his devotion to the principles of justice, fairness, and impartiality.

49. According to the preceding paragraph, what is the BEST action an officer can take in dealing with people in a neighborhood?

   A. Assist neighborhood residents by doing favors for them.
   B. Give special attention to the community leaders in order to be able to control them effectively.
   C. Behave in an appropriate manner and give all community members the same just treatment.
   D. Prepare a plan detailing what he, the officer, wants to do for the community and submit it for approval.

49._____

50. As used in the paragraph, the word *impartiality* means *most nearly*

   A. observant   B. unbiased
   C. righteousness   D. honesty

50._____

KEY (CORRECT ANSWERS)

1. B	11. B	21. A	31. D	41. C
2. B	12. A	22. C	32. C	42. C
3. A	13. C	23. B	33. C	43. D
4. A	14. D	24. D	34. C	44. D
5. D	15. B	25. A	35. A	45. A
6. C	16. B	26. D	36. C	46. A
7. D	17. A	27. C	37. A	47. C
8. C	18. B	28. A	38. C	48. B
9. D	19. D	29. A	39. B	49. C
10. C	20. B	30. B	40. C	50. B

TEST 2

DIRECTIONS: Each question or incomplete statement is followed by several suggested answers or completions. Select the one that BEST answers the question or completes the statement. *PRINT THE LETTER OF THE CORRECT ANSWER IN THE SPACE AT THE RIGHT.*

Questions 1-5.

DIRECTIONS: Questions 1 through 5 consist of short paragraphs. Each paragraph contains one word which is INCORRECTLY used because it is NOT in keeping with the meaning of the paragraph. Find the word in each paragraph which is INCORRECTLY used, and then select as the answer the suggested word which should be substituted for the incorrectly used word.

<u>SAMPLE QUESTION</u>

In determining who is to do the work in your unit, you will have to decide just who does what from day to day. One of your lowest responsibilities is to assign work so that everybody gets a fair share and that everyone can do his part well.
    A. new   B. old   C. important   D. performance

<u>EXPLANATION</u>

The word which is NOT in keeping with the meaning of the paragraph is "lowest". This is the INCORRECTLY used word. The suggested word "important" would be in keeping with the meaning of the paragraph and should be substituted for "lowest". Therefore, the CORRECT answer is Choice C.

1. If really good practice in the elimination of preventable injuries is to be achieved and held in any establishment, top management must refuse full and definite responsibility and must apply a good share of its attention to the task.

    A. accept   B. avoidable   C. duties   D. problem

2. Recording the human face for identification is by no means the only service performed by the camera in the field of investigation. When the trial of any issue takes place, a word picture is sought to be distorted to the court of incidents, occurrences, or events which are in dispute.

    A. appeals   B. description
    C. portrayed   D. deranged

3. In the collection of physical evidence, it cannot be emphasized too strongly that a haphazard systematic search at the scene of the crime is vital. Nothing must be overlooked. Often the only leads in a case will come from the results of this search.

    A. important   B. investigation
    C. proof   D. thorough

4. If an investigator has reason to suspect that the witness is mentally stable or a habitual drunkard, he should leave no stone unturned in his investigation to determine if the witness was under the influence of liquor or drugs, or was mentally unbalanced either at the time of the occurrence to which he testified or at the time of the trial.

    A. accused   B. clue   C. deranged   D. question

5. The use of records is a valuable step in crime investigation and is the main reason every department should maintain accurate reports. Crimes are not committed through the use of departmental records alone but from the use of all records, of almost every type, wherever they may be found and whenever they give any incidental information regarding the criminal.

    A. accidental   B. necessary   C. reported   D. solved

Questions 6-8.

DIRECTIONS: Questions 6 through 8 are to be answered SOLELY on the basis of the following passage.

The mass media are an integral part of the daily life of virtually every American. Among these media, the youngest, television, is the most persuasive. Ninety-five percent of American homes have at least one television set, and on the average that set is in use for about 40 hours each week. The central place of television in American life makes this medium the focal point of a growing national concern over the effects of media portrayals of violence on the values, attitudes, and behavior of an ever increasing audience.

In our concern about violence and its causes, it is easy to make television a scapegoat. But we emphasise the fact that there is no simple answer to the problem of violence -- no single explanation of its causes, and no single prescription for its control. It should be remembered that America also experienced high levels of crime and violence in periods before the advent of television.

The problem of balance, taste, and artistic merit in entertaining programs on television are complex. We cannot <u>countenance</u> government censorship of television. Nor would we seek to impose arbitrary limitations on programming which might jeopardize television's ability to deal in dramatic presentations with controversial social issues. Nonetheless, we are deeply troubled by television's constant portrayal of violence, not in any genuine attempt to focus artistic expression on the human condition, but rather in pandering to a public preoccupation with violence that television itself has helped to generate.

6. According to the passage, television uses violence MAINLY

    A. to highlight the reality of everyday existence
    B. to satisfy the audience's hunger for destructive action
    C. to shape the values and attitudes of the public
    D. when it films documentaries concerning human conflict

7. Which one of the following statements is BEST supported by this passage?

    A. Early American history reveals a crime pattern which is not related to television.
    B. Programs should give presentations of social issues and never portray violent acts.
    C. Television has proven that entertainment programs can easily make the balance between taste and artistic merit a simple matter.
    D. Values and behavior should be regulated by governmental censorship.

8. Of the following, which word has the same meaning as <u>countenance</u> as it is used in the above passage?

    A. approve   B. exhibit   C. oppose   D. reject

Questions 9-12.

DIRECTIONS: Questions 9 through 12 are to be answered SOLELY on the basis of the following graph relating to the burglary rate in the city, 2003 to 2008, inclusive.

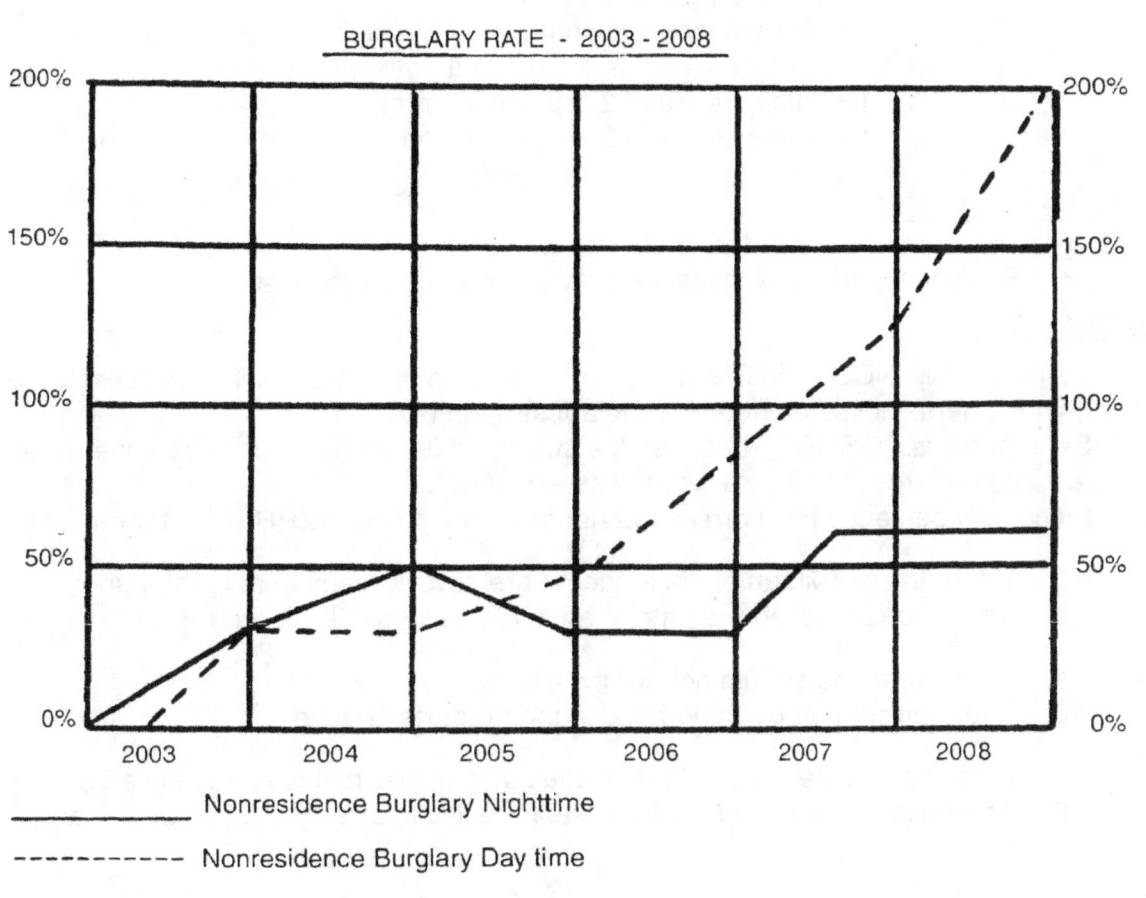

9. At the beginning of what year was the percentage increase in daytime and nighttime burglaries the SAME?

   A. 2004   B. 2005   C. 2006   D. 2008

10. In what year did the percentage of nighttime burglaries DECREASE?

    A. 2003   B. 2005   C. 2006   D. 2008

11. In what year was there the MOST rapid increase in the percentage of daytime non-residence burglaries?

    A. 2004   B. 2006   C. 2007   D. 2008

12. At the end of 2007, the actual number of nighttime burglaries committed

    A. was about 20%
    B. was 40%
    C. was 400
    D. cannot be determined from the information given

Questions 13-17.

DIRECTIONS: Questions 13 through 17 consist of two sentences numbered 1 and 2 taken from police officers' reports. Some of these sentences are correct according to ordinary formal English usage. Other sentences are incorrect because they contain errors in English usage or punctuation. Consider a sentence correct if it contains no errors in English usage or punctuation even if there may be other ways of writing the sentence correctly. Mark your answer to each question in the space at the right as follows:
- A. If only sentence 1 is correct, but not sentence 2
- B. If only sentence 2 is correct, but not sentence 1
- C. If sentences 1 and 2 are both correct
- D. If sentences 1 and 2 are both incorrect

SAMPLE QUESTION
1. The woman claimed that the purse was her's.
2. Everyone of the new officers was assigned to a patrol post.

EXPLANATION

Sentence 1 is INCORRECT because of an error in punctuation. The possessive words, "ours, yours, hers, theirs," do not have the apostrophe (').

Sentence 2 is CORRECT because the subject of the sentence is "Everyone" which is singular and requires the singular verb "was assigned".

Since only sentence 2 is correct, but not sentence 1, the CORRECT answer is B.

13. 1. Either the patrolman or his sergeant are always ready to help the public.   13.___
     2. The sergeant asked the patrolman when he would finish the report.

14. 1. The injured man could not hardly talk.   14.___
     2. Every officer had ought to hand in their reports on time.

15. 1. Approaching the victim of the assault, two large bruises were noticed by me.   15.___
     2. The prisoner was arrested for assault, resisting arrest, and use of a deadly weapon.

16. 1. A copy of the orders, which had been prepared by the captain, was given to each patrolman.   16.___
     2. It's always necessary to inform an arrested person of his constitutional rights before asking him any questions.

17. 1. To prevent further bleeding, I applied a tourniquet tothe wound.   17.___
     2. John Rano a senior officer was on duty at the time of the accident.

Questions 18-25.

DIRECTIONS: Answer each of Questions 18 through 25 SOLELY on the basis of the statement preceding the questions.

18. The criminal is one whose habits have been erroneously developed or, we should say, developed in anti-social patterns, and therefore the task of dealing with him is not one of punishment, but of treatment.   18.___
The basic principle expressed in this statement is BEST illustrated by the

A. emphasis upon rehabilitation in penal institutions
B. prevalence of capital punishment for murder
C. practice of imposing heavy fines for minor violations
D. legal provision for trial by jury in criminal cases

19. The writ of habeas corpus is one of the great guarantees of personal liberty. Of the following, the BEST justification for this statement is that the writ of habeas corpus is frequently used to

    A. compel the appearance in court of witnesses who are outside the state
    B. obtain the production of books and records at a criminal trial
    C. secure the release of a person improperly held in custody
    D. prevent the use of deception in obtaining testimony of reluctant witnesses

20. Fifteen persons suffered effects of carbon dioxide asphyxiation shortly before noon recently in a seventh-floor pressing shop. The accident occurred in a closed room where six steam presses were in operation. Four men and one woman were overcome.
    Of the following, the MOST probable reason for the fact that so many people were affected simultaneously is that

    A. women evidently show more resistance to the effects of carbon dioxide than men
    B. carbon dioxide is an odorless and colorless gas
    C. carbon dioxide is lighter than air
    D. carbon dioxide works more quickly at higher altitudes

21. Lay the patient on his stomach, one arm extended directly overhead, the other arm bent at the elbow, and with the face turned outward and resting on hand or forearm.
    To the officer who is skilled at administering first aid, these instructions should IMMEDIATELY suggest

    A. application of artificial respiration
    B. treatment for third degree burns of the arm
    C. setting a dislocated shoulder
    D. control of capillary bleeding in the stomach

22. The soda and acid fire extinguisher is the hand extinguisher most commonly used by officers. The main body of the cylinder is filled with a mixture of water and bicarbonate of soda. In a separate interior compartment, at the top, is a small bottle of sulphuric acid. When the extinguisher is inverted, the acid spills into the solution below and starts a chemical reaction. The carbon dioxide thereby generated forces the solution from the extinguisher.
    The officer who understands the operation of this fire extinguisher should know that it is LEAST likely to operate properly

    A. in basements or cellars
    B. in extremely cold weather
    C. when the reaction is of a chemical nature
    D. when the bicarbonate of soda is in solution

23. Suppose that, at a training lecture, you are told that many of the men in our penal institutions today are second and third offenders.
    Of the following, the MOST valid inference you can make SOLELY on the basis of this statement is that

    A. second offenders are not easily apprehended
    B. patterns of human behavior are not easily changed
    C. modern laws are not sufficiently flexible
    D. laws do not breed crimes

24. In all societies of our level of culture, acts are committed which arouse censure severe enough to take the form of punishment by the government. Such acts are crimes, not because of their inherent nature, but because of their ability to arouse resentment and to stimulate repressive measures.
Of the following, the MOST valid inference which can be drawn from this statement is that

    A. society unjustly punishes acts which are inherently criminal
    B. many acts are not crimes but are punished by society because such acts threaten the lives of innocent people
    C. only modern society has a level of culture
    D. societies sometimes disagree as to what acts are crimes

24.___

25. Crime cannot be measured directly. Its amount must be inferred from the frequency of some occurrence connected with it; for example, crimes brought to the attention of the police, persons arrested, prosecutions, convictions, and other dispositions, such as probation or commitment. Each of these may be used as an index of the amount of crime.
SOLELY on the basis of the foregoing statement, it is MOST correct to state that

    A. the incidence of crime cannot be estimated with any accuracy
    B. the number of commitments is usually greater than the number of probationary sentences
    C. the amount of crime is ordinarily directly correlated with the number of persons arrested
    D. a joint consideration of crimes brought to the attention of the police and the number of prosecutions undertaken gives little indication of the amount of crime in a locality

25.___

KEY (CORRECT ANSWERS)

1. B
2. A
3. D
4. C
5. D

6. B
7. A
8. A
9. A
10. B

11. D
12. D
13. D
14. D
15. B

16. C
17. A
18. A
19. C
20. B

21. A
22. B
23. B
24. D
25. C

SAFETY
EXAMINATION SECTION
TEST 1

DIRECTIONS: Each question or incomplete statement is followed by several suggested answers or completions. Select the one that BEST answers the question or completes the statement. *PRINT THE LETTER OF THE COREECT ANSWER IN THE SPACE AT THE RIGHT.*

1. When carrying pipe, employees are cautioned against lifting with the fingers inserted in the ends.
   The PROBABLE reason for this caution is to avoid the possibility of

   A. dropping and damaging pipe
   B. getting dirt and perspiration on the inside of the pipe
   C. cutting the fingers on the edge of the pipe
   D. straining finger muscles

2. The MOST common cause for a workman to lose his balance and fall when working from an extension ladder is

   A. too much spring in the ladder
   B. sideways sliding of the top
   C. exerting a heavy pull on an object which gives suddenly
   D. working on something directly behind the ladder

3. It is NOT necessary to wear protective goggles when

   A. drilling rivet holes in a steel beam
   B. sharpening tools on a power grinder
   C. welding a steel plate to a pipe column
   D. laying up a cinder block partition

4. On your first day on the job as a helper, you are assigned to work with a maintainer. During the course of the work, you realize that the maintainer is about to violate a basic safety rule.
   In this case, the BEST thing for you to do is to

   A. immediately call it to his attention
   B. say nothing until he actually violates the rule and then call it to his attention
   C. say nothing, but later report this action to the foreman
   D. walk away from him so that you will not become involved

5. Telephones are located alongside of the tracks for emergency use. The locations of these telephones are indicated by blue lights.
   The reason for selecting this color rather than green is that

   A. a blue light can be seen for greater distances
   B. blue lights are easier to buy
   C. green cannot be seen by a person who is color-blind
   D. green lights are used for train signals

6. If it is necessary to lift up and hold one heavy part of a piece of equipment with a pinch bar so that there is enough clearance to work with the hands under the part, one IMPORTANT precaution is to

   A. wear gloves
   B. watch the bar to be ready if it slips
   C. work as fast as possible
   D. insert a temporary block to hold the part

7. The MOST important reason for insisting on neatness in maintenance quarters is that it

   A. increases the available storage space
   B. makes for good employee morale
   C. prevents tools from becoming rusty
   D. decreases the chances of accidents to employees

8. There are many steel ladders and stairways for the use of maintenance workers. Their GREATEST danger is that they

   A. have sharp edges causing cuts
   B. are slippery when greasy and wet
   C. cause colds
   D. have no *give* and thus cause fatigue

9. When using a brace and bit to bore a hole completely through a partition, it is MOST important to

   A. lean heavily on the brace and bit
   B. maintain a steady turning speed all through the job
   C. have the body in a position that will not be easily thrown off balance
   D. reverse the direction of the bit at frequent intervals

10. Flux is used when soldering two pieces of sheet metal together in order to

    A. conduct the heat of the soldering iron to the sheets
    B. lower the melting point of the solder
    C. glue the solder to the sheets
    D. protect the sheet metal from oxidizing when heated by the soldering iron

11. A rule of the transit system states that in walking on the track, walk opposite the direction of traffic on that track if possible.
    By logical reasoning, the PRINCIPAL safety idea behind this rule is that the man on the track

    A. is more likely to see an approaching train
    B. will be seen more readily by the motorman
    C. need not be as careful
    D. is better able to judge the speed of the train

12. An outstanding cause of accidents is the improper use of tools.
    The MOST helpful conclusion you can draw from this statement is that

    A. most tools are defective
    B. many accidents involving the use of tools occur because of poor working habits

C. most workers are poorly trained
D. many accidents involving the use of tools are unavoidable

13. An employee is required to make a written report of any unusual occurrence promptly. The BEST reason for requiring promptness is that

    A. it helps prevent similar occurrences
    B. the employee is less likely to forget details
    C. there is always a tendency to do a better job under pressure
    D. the report may be too long if made at an employee"s convenience

14. There are a few workers who are seemingly prone to accidents and who, regardless of their assigned job, have a higher accident rate than the average worker.
    If your co-worker is known to be such an individual, the BEST course for you to pursue would be to

    A. do most of the assigned work yourself
    B. refuse to work with this individual
    C. provide him with a copy of all rules and regulations
    D. personally check all safety precautions on each job

15. When summoning an ambulance for an injured person, it is MOST important to give the

    A. name of the injured person
    B. nature of the injuries
    C. cause of the accident
    D. location of the injured person

16. The MOST likely cause of accidents involving minor injuries is

    A. careless work practices
    B. lack of safety devices
    C. inferior equipment and materials
    D. insufficient safety posters

17. In an accident report, the information which may be MOST useful in decreasing the recurrence of similar-type accidents is the

    A. extent of injuries sustained
    B. time the accident happened
    C. number of people involved
    D. cause of the accident

18. Before a newly-riveted connection can be approved, the rivets should be struck with a light hammer in order to

    A. improve the shape of the rivet heads
    B. knock off any rust or burnt metal
    C. detect any loose rivets
    D. give the rivets a tighter fit

19. If the feet of a ladder are found to be resting on a slightly uneven surface, it would be BEST to

    A. move the ladder to an entirely different location
    B. even up the feet of the ladder with a small wedge
    C. get two men to bolster the ladder while it is being climbed
    D. get another ladder that is more suitable to the conditions

20. It would be POOR practice to hold a piece of wood in your hands or lap while you are tightening a screw in the wood because

    A. the wood would probably split
    B. sufficient leverage cannot be obtained
    C. the screwdriver may bend
    D. you might injure yourself

21. If a man on a job has to report an accident to the office by telephone, he should request the name of the person taking the call and also note the time.
    The reason for this precaution is to fix responsibility for the

    A. entire handling of the accident thereafter
    B. accuracy of the report
    C. recording of the report
    D. preparation of the final written report

22. Employees of the transit system whose work requires them to enter upon the tracks are warned not to wear loose-fitting clothes.
    The MOST important reason for this warning is that loose-fitting clothes may

    A. tear more easily than snug-fitting clothes
    B. give insufficient protection against dust
    C. catch on some projection of a passing train
    D. interfere when the men are using heavy tools

23. In case of accident, employees who witnessed the accident are required to make INDIVIDUAL written reports on prescribed forms as soon as possible.
    The MOST logical reason for requiring such individual reports rather than a single, joint report signed by all witnesses is that the individual reports are

    A. *less* likely to be lost at the same time
    B. *more* likely to result in reducing the number of accidents
    C. *less* likely to contain unnecessary information
    D. *more* likely to give the complete picture

24. The logical reason that certain employees who work on the tracks carry small parts in fiber pails rather than in steel pails is that fiber pails

    A. can't be dented by rough usage
    B. do not conduct electricity
    C. are stronger
    D. can't rust

25. Maintenance workers whose duties require them to work on the tracks generally work in pairs.
The LEAST likely of the following possible reasons for this practice is that

    A. the men can help each other in case of accident
    B. it protects against vandalism
    C. some of the work requires two men
    D. there is usually too much equipment for one man to carry

25.____

KEY (CORRECT ANSWERS)

1.	C	11.	A
2.	C	12.	B
3.	D	13.	B
4.	A	14.	D
5.	D	15.	D
6.	D	16.	A
7.	D	17.	D
8.	B	18.	C
9.	C	19.	B
10.	D	20.	D

21.	C
22.	C
23.	D
24.	B
25.	B

TEST 2

DIRECTIONS: Each question or incomplete statement is followed by several suggested answers or completions. Select the one that BEST answers the question or completes the statement. *PRINT THE LETTER OF THE CORRECT ANSWER IN THE SPACE AT THE RIGHT.*

1. Safety-mindedness cannot be achieved by command; it must be developed. Assume that you will be responsible for informing and training your subordinates in proper safety procedures.
   Which of the following methods is the MOST effective means of developing proper concern for safety among your subordinates?

   A. Award prizes for the best safety slogans
   B. Issue monthly safety bulletins
   C. Establish a safety suggestion program
   D. Hold periodic, informal group meetings on safety

   1._____

2. Of the following, the MAIN purpose of a safety training program for employees is to

   A. fix the blame for accidents
   B. describe accidents which have occurred
   C. hold the employees responsible for unsafe working conditions
   D. make the employees aware of the basic causes of accidents

   2._____

3. When administering first aid to a person suffering from shock as a result of an accident, of the following, it is MOST important to

   A. cover the person and keep him warm
   B. apply artificial respiration
   C. prop him up in a sitting position
   D. massage the person in order to aid blood circulation

   3._____

4. Assume you have just been appointed. You notice that certain equipment which is assigned to you is defective and that use of this equipment may eventually result in unnecessary costs and perhaps injury to you.
   The BEST thing for you to do is to

   A. speak to the maintenance men in the project about repairing the equipment
   B. discuss the matter with your foreman
   C. mind your own business since you have just been appointed
   D. speak to other workers and find out if they had any experience with defective equipment

   4._____

5. Assume you are working in a project building and one of the housing caretakers has just been seriously injured in an accident in the slop sink room.
   Your FIRST concern should be to

   A. help the injured man
   B. find the cause of the accident
   C. report the accident to your foreman
   D. report the accident to the caretaker's boss

   5._____

6. Assume a mass of extension cords plugged into one outlet in a shop results in overloading the electrical circuit and causes a fire.
   Which of the following types of extinguisher should be used to put out the fire?

   A. Carbon dioxide (CO_2)
   B. Water
   C. Soda acid
   D. Carbon tetrachloride

7. Manufacturers of chemicals usually recommend that special precautions be taken when the chemicals are used.
   Of the following, which one would a manufacturer be LEAST likely to recommend?

   A. Wear leather gloves
   B. Wear a respirator
   C. Wear safety goggles
   D. Have a first aid kit available

Questions 8-10.

DIRECTIONS: Questions 8 through 10 consist of groups of statements that have to do with safety precautions and procedures. Choose the statement in each group that is NOT correct.

8. A. The label on the original container of the pesticide should be read before each use.
    B. Pest control equipment should be cleaned regularly.
    C. Whenever there is a choice of chemicals, the chemical which is less hazardous to humans should be used at all times.
    D. For the transfer of concentrates from drums, either threaded taps or drum pumps should be used.

9. A. Do not use a petroleum base on an asphalt tile floor.
    B. Do not spray oil base sprays on material colored with oil soluble dyes.
    C. Do not use respirators.
    D. Do not use pesticides which are highly poisonous to mammals.

10. (The following statements deal with disposal of empty containers which hold highly toxic organic phosphate insecticides.)

    A. Do not reuse these containers.
    B. Pour one pint of water into the empty container, add bicarbonate of soda, and bury the container of rinse solution at least 18 inches below ground.
    C. Wet all inner surfaces with the proper rinse solution.
    D. Punch holes in the top and bottom of the can, crush the can, and bury deeply in an isolated location.

11. A good first-aid treatment to administer to a man who has apparently been rendered unconscious by a high voltage shock would be to

    A. give him a stimulant by mouth
    B. apply artificial respiration if he is not breathing
    C. apply artificial respiration as a precautionary measure even if he is breathing
    D. keep him warm and comfortable

12. A contributing cause present in practically all accidents is

    A. failure to give close attention to the job at hand
    B. lack of cooperation among the men in a gang
    C. failure to place the right man in the right job
    D. use of improper tools

13. Safety requires that wood ladders be unpainted.
    The PROBABLE reason for this is that paint

    A. is inflammable
    B. may deteriorate wood
    C. makes ladder rungs slippery
    D. may cover cracks or defects

14. If you notice one of your helpers doing a job in an unsafe manner and he tells you that this is the way the maintainer told him to do it, you should FIRST

    A. speak to this maintainer and find out if the helper was telling you the truth
    B. reprimand the helper for violating safety rules
    C. question this maintainer to see if he knows the safe way to do the job
    D. show the helper the correct method and see that he does the job properly

15. If a person has a deep puncture in his finger caused by a sharp nail, the BEST immediate first-aid procedure would be to

    A. encourage bleeding by exerting pressure around the injured area
    B. stop all bleeding
    C. prevent air from reaching the wound
    D. probe the wound for steel particles

16. It is MOST important to give complete details of an accident on the accident report because this will

    A. cause the injured employee to be more careful in the future
    B. keep supervision informed of the working conditions
    C. help in the defense against spurious compensation claims
    D. provide information to help avoid future accidents

17. A transit employee equipped with only a white flashlight, who wishes to stop a train because of an emergency, should face the train and wave the light in a

    A. vertical line
    B. vertical circle
    C. horizontal line
    D. forward and backward direction

18. The employee who opens a first-aid kit must make an immediate report on a prescribed form.
    Such report would NOT show the

    A. name of the employee opening the kit
    B. last previous date on which the kit was used

C. purpose for which the materials therein were used
D. amount of first aid material used

19. Carbon tetrachloride fire extinguishers have been replaced by dry chemical fire extinguishers MAINLY because the carbon tetrachloride is

   A. toxic
   B. not as effective
   C. frequently pilfered for cleaning purposes
   D. not readily available

20. The BEST first-aid for a man who has no external injury but is apparently suffering from internal injury due to an accident is to

   A. take him immediately to a doctor's office
   B. administer a stimulant
   C. cover him with a blanket and immediately summon a doctor or ambulance
   D. administer artificial respiration

21. While your men were working on the plumbing of a station toilet, a passenger tripped over some of your material on the platform.
In making a report of the accident, the LEAST necessary item to include is the

   A. time of day
   B. distance from the entrance turnstile to the toilet
   C. date of occurrence
   D. condition of the platform when the accident occurred

22. All employees witnessing an accident are required to make a written report as soon as possible describing what they witnessed.
The MOST likely reason for requiring these reports in writing and as soon as possible is to

   A. make sure no witnesses are overlooked
   B. be able to correct the reports without delay
   C. get as many facts as possible on record before they are forgotten
   D. relieve supervision of the time consuming job of verbally questioning all witnesses

23. Of the following, the type of fire extinguisher which should be used on electrical fires is the _____ type.

   A. foam   B. soda-acid
   C. pumped-water   D. dry chemical

24. The PRIMARY purpose of an emergency alarm is to

   A. test circuits to see if they are alive
   B. provide a means of removing power from the third rail
   C. inform the trainmaster that trains cannot run in his zone
   D. inform maintenance crews working on the tracks that an emergency exists

25. In regard to flagging signals, which of the following statements is TRUE?　　25._____
  A. A red flag must never be used to give a proceed signal to a motorman.
  B. Under all conditions, only a red flag or lamp can be used as a signal to the motorman to stop the train.
  C. After stopping a train, if a flagman wishes to signal the motorman to resume his normal speed, he should wave a yellow flag.
  D. Under normal flagging conditions, moving a white light up and down slowly is a signal to the motorman to resume normal speed and that the motorman should be prepared to stop within his range of vision.

KEY (CORRECT ANSWERS)

1.	D	11.	B
2.	D	12.	A
3.	A	13.	D
4.	B	14.	D
5.	A	15.	A
6.	A	16.	D
7.	A	17.	C
8.	C	18.	B
9.	C	19.	A
10.	B	20.	C

21. B
22. C
23. D
24. B
25. A

EXAMINATION SECTION
TEST 1

DIRECTIONS: Each question or incomplete statement is followed by several suggested answers or completions. Select the one that BEST answers the question or completes the statement. *PRINT THE LETTER OF THE CORRECT ANSWER IN THE SPACE AT THE RIGHT.*

1. According to the American Red Cross, the proper IMMEDIATE first aid care for a frost-bitten hand is to

    A. rub the hand with snow
    B. place the part in warm water
    C. cover the hand with a woolen cloth
    D. vigorously rub the hands together

    1._____

2. The symptoms of heat exhaustion are

    A. pale, clammy skin, low temperature, weak pulse
    B. rapid and strong pulse, dry skin, high temperature
    C. headache, red face, unconsciousness
    D. abdominal cramps, red skin, profuse sweating

    2._____

3. Arterial pressure points

    A. are best located by taking the pulse
    B. lie close to bones near the surface of the body
    C. are used to cut off all blood circulation
    D. are deepseated and require great pressure

    3._____

4. Of the following, the one NOT recommended for the first aid of burns is

    A. boric acid   B. baking soda
    C. petrolatum ointment   D. Epsom salts

    4._____

5. A person who has fainted should be

    A. propped up on a pillow or head rest
    B. given a warm drink
    C. aroused as soon as possible
    D. laid flat and kept quiet

    5._____

6. Of the following associations of symptom(s) and sudden illness or accident, the INCORRECT one is

    A. blood spurting from the wrist - cut artery
    B. stoppage of breathing - suffocation
    C. pale, cold, moist skin - shock
    D. partial tearing of ligaments of a joint - strain

    6._____

7. In the care of a sprained ankle, an INCORRECT procedure in first aid would be to

    A. elevate the sprained part   B. apply cold applications
    C. massage the part to restore circulation D. apply a temporary support

    7._____

8. In administering first aid, one should encourage bleeding by mild pressure, being careful not to bruise the tissue, in wounds classified as

   A. punctures   B. incisions   C. lacerations   D. abrasions

9. All of the following first aid rules for simple nosebleeds may be safely followed EXCEPT

   A. gently pinching the nostrils together
   B. applying cold compresses to the nose
   C. blowing the nose gently after bleeding stops to remove blood clots
   D. inserting a plug of absorbent cotton in each of the nostrils

10. Of the following associations of symptom and illness, the one which is INCORRECT is

    A. cough - onset of measles
    B. pallor - anemia
    C. sore throat - impetigo
    D. red eyes, accompanied by a discharge - conjunctivitis

KEY (CORRECT ANSWERS)

1. C   6. D
2. A   7. C
3. B   8. A
4. A   9. C
5. D   10. C

TEST 2

DIRECTIONS: Each question or incomplete statement is followed by several suggested answers or completions. Select the one that BEST answers the question or completes the statement. *PRINT THE LETTER OF THE CORRECT ANSWER IN THE SPACE AT THE RIGHT.*

1. The MAJORITY of home accidents result from 1.____
   A. burns   B. suffocation   C. falls   D. poisons

2. Of the following, the one that is NOT a symptom of shock is 2.____
   A. flushed face
   B. weak pulse
   C. cold, clammy skin
   D. feeling of weakness

3. The purpose of applying artificial respiration to the victim of an electric shock is to 3.____
   A. restore blood circulation
   B. avoid excessive loss of blood
   C. keep the victim warm
   D. supply oxygen to the lungs

4. The INCORRECT procedure in treating nosebleeds is to 4.____
   A. have the victim lie down immediately
   B. apply a large cold, wet cloth to the nose
   C. pack the nose gently with gauze
   D. press the nostrils firmly together

5. In one minute, the heart of a normal man who is resting beats APPROXIMATELY _____ times. 5.____
   A. 30   B. 72   C. 98   D. 112

6. In attempting to revive a person who has stopped breathing after receiving an electric shock, it is MOST important to 6.____
   A. start artificial respiration immediately
   B. wrap the victim in a blanket
   C. massage the ankles and wrists
   D. force the victim to swallow a stimulant

7. In the Holger-Nielsen method of artificial respiration, the victim is placed 7.____
   A. on his stomach
   B. on his back
   C. in a kneeling position
   D. in any comfortable position

8. Frequent deaths are reported as a result of running an automobile engine in a closed garage. 8.____
   Death results from
   A. suffocation
   B. carbon monoxide poisoning
   C. excessive humidity
   D. an excess of carbon dioxide in the air

9. Fever, chills, inflamed eyelids, running nose, and cough are symptoms of 9.____

    A. measles   B. chicken pox
    C. tuberculosis   D. scarlet fever

10. Among the usual signs of measles are listlessness, red watery eyes that are sensitive to light, a moderate fever, and 10.____

    A. a running nose   B. a blotchy red rash
    C. a running ear   D. convulsions

KEY (CORRECT ANSWERS)

1.	C	6.	A
2.	A	7.	A
3.	D	8.	B
4.	A	9.	A
5.	B	10.	A

TEST 3

DIRECTIONS: Each question or incomplete statement is followed by several suggested answers or completions. Select the one that BEST answers the question or completes the statement. *PRINT THE LETTER OF THE CORRECT ANSWER IN THE SPACE AT THE RIGHT.*

1. To provide transit employees with quick assistance in the case of minor injuries, it would be MOST logical to   1._____

    A. instruct the employees in first aid techniques
    B. provide each employee with a first aid kit
    C. have one centrally located medical office for the transit system
    D. equip all employees with walkie-talkie devices

2. If a person has just received an electric shock and appears dead, the FIRST two things that a rescuer should do in proper order are: 2._____

    A. Wrap the victim in a blanket and free him from the circuit
    B. Free the victim from the circuit and wrap him in a blanket
    C. Free the victim from the circuit and give him a stimulant
    D. Free the victim from the circuit and apply artificial respiration

3. In the back pressure, arm-lift method of artificial respiration, each full cycle should be administered steadily at a rate per minute of   3._____

    A. 12 to 15 times   B. 70 to 80 times
    C. 20 to 30 times   D. once

4. During an epileptic seizure, the patient should be   4._____

    A. given a drink of water or stimulant
    B. held securely so that he will not struggle
    C. carried to the medical office immediately
    D. left where he has fallen and prevented from injuring himself

5. When a person suffers a compound fracture of the leg, in all probability the damaged bone is the   5._____

    A. radius or ulna   B. clavicle
    C. sternum   D. tibia or fibula

6. The overall purpose of the application of heat to a victim in shock is to   6._____

    A. cause sweating
    B. prevent a large loss of body heat
    C. increase the body's temperature
    D. increase the blood circulation

7. The American Red Cross recommends that an abrasion be treated by   7._____

    A. applying iodine
    B. covering the wound with gauze
    C. washing the wound with soap and water
    D. applying mercurochrome

8. Of the following, the symptom of heatstroke MOST frequently noted is

    A. an absence of perspiration
    B. mental confusion
    C. headache
    D. dilated pupils

9. A puncture wound is considered serious from the point of view that

    A. bleeding may be hard to stop
    B. injury to tissue may be extensive
    C. infection is likely to result
    D. multiple injury may result

10. The method of resuscitation MOST generally accepted today is the _____ method.

    A. back pressure arm lift   B. mouth to mouth
    C. Sylvester   D. Schaefer

KEY (CORRECT ANSWERS)

1. A   6. B
2. D   7. C
3. A   8. A
4. D   9. C
5. D   10. B

TEST 4

DIRECTIONS: Each question or incomplete statement is followed by several suggested answers or completions. Select the one that BEST answers the question or completes the statement. *PRINT THE LETTER OF THE CORRECT ANSWER IN THE SPACE AT THE RIGHT.*

1. Suppose that, as a uniformed officer, you are called to administer first aid to an unconscious person.
   Of the following, the BEST reason for NOT attempting to administer a liquid stimulant to this person is that

   A. he may have poor circulation of blood
   B. he may choke on the liquid
   C. stimulants affect the heart
   D. stimulants should be administered at the direction of a physician

   1.____

2. Assume that it is necessary for you to apply a tourniquet in order to stop serious bleeding.
   The one of the following MOST properly used for this purpose is

   A. thin cord   B. thick rope   C. a necktie   D. wire

   2.____

3. Suppose that an elderly man has met with an accident and is lying on the floor awaiting the arrival of a doctor. Of the following, the BEST action to take in order to prevent shock is to

   A. raise him to a sitting position
   B. apply a wet cloth to his head
   C. apply artificial respiration
   D. cover him with a coat

   3.____

4. While you are on duty, a fellow officer suddenly turns pale and his breathing becomes rapid and shallow. He is apparently suffering from heat exhaustion.
   Of the following, the LEAST desirable action for you to take under the circumstances is to

   A. apply cold cloths to his head
   B. place him in a reclining position
   C. give him a stimulant
   D. have him sip salt water

   4.____

5. Assume that a fellow officer is in contact with an electrically charged wire.
   Of the following, the BEST reason for NOT grasping the victim's clothing with your bare hands in order to pull him off the wire is that

   A. his clothing may be damp with perspiration
   B. his clothing may be 100% wool
   C. you may be standing on a dry surface
   D. you may be wearing rubber-soled shoes

   5.____

6. Suppose a man falls from a two-story high scaffold and is unconscious. You should

   A. call for medical assistance and avoid moving the man
   B. get someone to help you move him indoors to a bed
   C. have someone help you walk him around until he revives
   D. hold his head up and pour a stimulant down his throat

7. For proper first aid treatment, a person who has fainted should be

   A. doused with cold water and then warmly covered
   B. given artificial respiration until he is revived
   C. laid down with his head lower than the rest of his body
   D. slapped on the face until he is revived

8. If you are called on to give first aid to a person who is suffering from shock, you should

   A. apply cold towels   B. give him a stimulant
   C. keep him awake   D. wrap him warmly

9. Artificial respiration would NOT be proper first aid for a person suffering from

   A. drowning   B. electric shock
   C. external bleeding   D. suffocation

10. Suppose you are called on to give first aid to several victims of an accident. First attention should be given to the one who is

    A. bleeding severely   B. groaning loudly
    C. unconscious   D. vomiting

KEY (CORRECT ANSWERS)

1. B   6. A
2. C   7. C
3. D   8. D
4. A   9. C
5. A   10. A

TEST 5

DIRECTIONS: Each question or incomplete statement is followed by several suggested answers or completions. Select the one that BEST answers the question or completes the statement. *PRINT THE LETTER OF THE CORRECT ANSWER IN THE SPACE AT THE RIGHT.*

1. Suppose that, while you are on patrol, a teenage boy dashes out of a dry cleaning store, his clothes afire.
   The BEST action for you to take in this situation is to

   A. stop the boy and roll him in a coat to smother the flames
   B. lead the boy quickly to the nearest store and douse him with large quantities of water
   C. remove all burning articles of clothing from the boy as quickly as possible
   D. take the boy back into the dry cleaning store where a fire extinguisher will almost certainly be available to extinguish the flames quickly

   1.____

2. A woman comes running towards you crying that her child was bitten by their pet dog.
   The FIRST action you should take is to

   A. summon a doctor so that he may treat the wounds
   B. shoot the dog to prevent it from biting others
   C. have the child put to bed
   D. apply ice packs to the wounds until the pain subsides

   2.____

3. You are called to an apartment house to stop a quarrel between a husband and wife. When you arrive there, you find that the husband has left and that the woman is lying unconscious on the floor. In the meantime, a neighbor has telephoned for an ambulance.
   You note that the room temperature is about 50°.
   The FIRST action is to

   A. rub the hands of the woman to keep her blood circulating
   B. make her drink hot tea or coffee to try to revive her
   C. place a hot water bottle under her feet to keep them warm
   D. place one blanket underneath her and another one over her

   3.____

4. As a person who is well-informed in the fundamentals of giving first aid, you should know that the *Schaefer Method* is MOST helpful for

   A. stopping bleeding
   B. transporting injured persons
   C. promoting respiration
   D. stopping the spread of infection

   4.____

5. While you are on duty, a middle-aged man crossing the street cries out with pain, presses his hands to his chest, and stands perfectly still. You suspect that he may have suffered a heart attack.
   You should

   A. ask him to cross the street quickly in order to prevent his being hit by moving traffic
   B. permit him to lie down flat in the street while you divert the traffic

   5.____

93

C. ask him for the name of his doctor so that you can summon him
D. request a cab to take him to the nearest hospital for immediate treatment

6. When administering first aid for the accidental swallowing of poison, water is given CHIEFLY to

   A. increase energy
   B. quiet the nerves
   C. weaken the poison
   D. prevent choking

7. The CHIEF purpose of administering artificial respiration to first aid is to

   A. exert regular pressure on the heart
   B. force the blood into circulation by pressure
   C. force air into the lungs
   D. keep the person warm by keeping his body in motion

8. When severe shock occurs, it is important for the person being treated to have

   A. sedatives and cold drinks
   B. warmth and low head position
   C. hot drinks and much activity
   D. sedatives and sitting position

9. When administering first aid, a tourniquet is used to

   A. sterilize the injured area
   B. hold the splits in place
   C. hold the dressing in place
   D. stop the loss of blood

10. Heat exhaustion and sunstroke are alike in that in both cases the person affected

    A. has hot dry skin and a red face
    B. should lie with head high
    C. should be given stimulants
    D. has been exposed to heat

KEY (CORRECT ANSWERS)

1. A
2. A
3. D
4. C
5. B

6. C
7. C
8. B
9. D
10. D

REPORT WRITING

EXAMINATION SECTION

TEST 1

DIRECTIONS: Each question or incomplete statement is followed by several suggested answers or completions. Select the one that BEST answers the question or completes the statement. *PRINT THE LETTER OF THE CORRECT ANSWER IN THE SPACE AT THE RIGHT.*

Questions 1-5.

DIRECTIONS: Questions 1 through 5 are to be answered SOLELY on the basis of the following report.

REPORT OF DEFECTIVE EQUIPMENT

DEPARTMENT: *Social Services* REPORT NO. 3026
DIVISION: *Personnel* DATE OF REPORT: *5/27*
ROOM: 120B

DEFECTIVE EQUIPMENT: *Six office telephones with pick-up and hold buttons*

DESCRIPTION OF DEFECT: *Marjorie Black, a Clerk, called on 5/22 to report that the button lights for the four lines on all six telephones in her office were not functioning and it was, therefore, impossible to know which lines were in use. On 5/26, Howard Perl, Admin. Asst., called in regard to the same telephones. He was annoyed because no repairs had been made and stated that all the employees in his unit were being inconvenienced. He requested prompt repair service.*

Ruth Gomez
SIGNATURE OF REPORTING EMPLOYEE
Sr. Telephone Operator
TITLE

JUDITH O'LAUGHLIN
SIGNATURE OF SUPERVISOR   TO BE COMPLETED AFTER SERVICING
DATE: 5/28
APPROVED: *Judy O'Laughlin*

---

1. The person who made a written report about the improper functioning of telephones in the Personnel division is
   A. Marjorie Black   B. Ruth Gomez
   C. Howard Perl   D. Judith O'Laughlin

1.____

2. How many days elapsed between the original request for telephone repair service and the completion of service? 2.____
   A. 2   B. 4   C. 5   D. 6

3. Of the following, the only information NOT given in the report is 3.____
   A. number of employees affected by the defective service
   B. number of the report
   C. number of telephones with a button defect
   D. telephone numbers of the defective phones

4. The one of the following items of information which would have been LEAST helpful to the repairman who was assigned this repair job is that 4.____
   A. the defect involved pick-up buttons for 4 serviced lines
   B. the location is Room 120B in the Department of Social Services
   C. Marjorie Black initially reported the defective equipment
   D. six telephone units need to be repaired

5. Which of the following statements is CORRECT concerning the people mentioned in the report? 5.____
   A. Ruth Gomez has a higher titled than Judith O'Laughlin
   B. Judith O'Laughlin's signature appears twice on this form
   C. Howard Perl reported on May 25 that the telephones needed adjusting
   D. Marjorie Black reported that she was disturbed that no repairs had been made

Questions 6-10.

DIRECTIONS: Questions 6 through 10 are based on the UNUSUAL OCCURRENCE REPORT given below. Five phrases in the report have been removed and are listed below the report as 1. through 5. in each of the five places where phrases of the report have been left out, the number of a question has been inserted. For each question, select the number of the missing phrase which would make the report read correctly.

UNUSUAL OCCURRENCE REPORT

POST _____
TOUR _____
DATE _____

Location of Occurrence:_____
REMARKS: While making rounds this morning, I thought that I heard some strange sounds coming from Storeroom #55. Upon investigation, I saw that <u>6</u> and that the door to the storeroom was slightly opened. At 2:45 A.M. I <u>7</u>.

Suddenly two men jumped out from <u>8</u>, dropped the tools which they were holding, and made a dash for the door. I ordered them to stop, but they just kept running.

3 (#1)

I was able to get a good look at both of them. One man was wearing a green jacket and had a full beard, and the other was short and had blond hair. Immediately, I called the police; and about two minutes later, I notified 9. I 10 the police arrived, and I gave them the complete details of the incident.

                                          Security Officer Donald Rimson   23807
                                                               Signature   Pass No.

1. the special inspection control desk
2. behind some crates
3. the lock had been tampered with
4. remained at the storeroom unit
5. entered the storeroom and began to look around

6.   A. 1   B. 3   C. 4   D. 5   6.____

7.   A. 2   B. 3   C. 4   D. 5   7.____

8.   A. 1   B. 2   C. 3   D. 4   8.____

9.   A. 1   B. 2   C. 3   D. 4   9.____

10. A. 2   B. 3   C. 4   D. 5   10.____

Questions 11-13.

DIRECTIONS: Below is a report consisting of 15 numbered sentences, some of which are not consistent with the principles of good report writing. Questions 11 through 13 are to be answered SOLELY on the basis of the information contained in the report and your knowledge of investigative principles and practices.

To: Tom Smith, Administrative Investigator
From: John Jones, Supervising Investigator

1. On January 7, I received a call from Mrs. H. Harris of 684 Sunset Street, Brooklyn.
2. Mr. Harris informed me that she wanted to report an instance of fraud relating to public assistance payments being received by her neighbor, Mrs. I Wallace.
3. I advised her that such a subject would best be discussed in person.
4. I then arranged a field visitation for January 10 at Mrs. Harris' apartment, 684 Sunset Street, Brooklyn.
5. On January 10, I discussed the basis for Mrs. Harris' charge against Mrs. Wallace at the former's apartment.
6. She stated that her neighbor is receiving Aid to Dependent Children payments for seven children, but that only three of her children are still living with her.
7. In addition, Mrs. Harris also claimed that her husband, whom she reported to the authorities as missing, usually sees her several times a week.
8. After further questioning, Mrs. Harris admitted to me that she had been quite friendly with Mrs. Wallace until they recently argued about trash left in their adjoining hall corridor.

9. However, she firmly stated that her allegations against Mrs. Wallace were valid and that she feared repercussions for her actions.
10. At the completion of the interview, I assured Mrs. Harris of the confidentiality of her statements and that an attempt would be made to verify her allegations.
11. As I was leaving Mrs. Harris' apartment, I noticed a man, aged approximately 45, walking out of Mrs. Wallace's apartment.
12. I followed him until he entered an old green Oldsmobile and sped away.
13. On January 3, I returned to 684 Sunset Court, having determined that Mrs. Wallace is receiving assistance as indicated by Mrs. Harris.
14. However, upon presentation of official identification Mrs. Wallace refused to admit me to her apartment or grant an interview.
15. I am therefore referring this matter to you for further instructions.

John Jones
Supervising Investigator

11. The one of the following statements that clearly lacks vital information is Statement
    A. 8   B. 10   C. 12   D. 14

12. Which of the following sentences from the report is ambiguous?
    A. 2   B. 3   C. 7   D. 10

13. Which of the following sentences contains information contradicting other data in the above report? Sentence
    A. 3   B. 8   C. 10   D. 13

Questions 14-16.

DIRECTIONS: Questions 14 through 16 are to be answered on the basis of the following report.

To: Ralph King
    Senior Menagerie Keeper

Date: April 3
Subject:

From: William Rattner
      Menagerie Keeper

This memorandum is to inform you of the disappearance of the boa constrictor from the Reptile Collection in the Main Building.

This morning upon entering the room, I realized that the snake was missing. After having asked around, I am of the opinion that the boa constrictor has been stolen. Since there are no signs of forced entry, it seems likely that whoever removed the snake from the premises entered the room through a window which had been left unlocked the previous night. I, therefore, suggest that all zoo personnel be more concerned with proper security measures in the future so that something like this does not happen again.

14. Which one of the following pieces of information has been OMITTED from the report by the Menagerie Keeper?
    A. Action taken by him after his discovery that the boa constrictor was missing
    B. The date that the disappearance of the boa constrictor was noted
    C. The time that the disappearance of the boa constrictor was noted
    D. The building in which the boa constrictor was kept

14.____

15. Based upon information contained in the above paragraph, which of the following statements would be BEST as the subject of this report?
    A. Request for more effective security measures in the oo
    B. Vandalism in the zoo
    C. Disappearance of boa constrictor
    D. Request for replacement of boa constrictor

15.____

16. According to the above report, which of the following statements CANNOT be considered factual?
    A. The boa constrictor was being kept in the Main Building
    B. The boa constrictor is missing
    C. All zoo personnel are careless about security measures
    D. There are no signs of forced entry

16.____

Questions 17-19.

DIRECTIONS: Questions 17 through 19 are to be answered on the basis of the Accident Report below. Read this report carefully before answering the questions. Select your answers ONLY on the basis of this report.

ACCIDENT REPORT

February 14

On February 14 at 3:45 P.M., Mr. Warren, while on the top of a stairway at the 34th Street Station, realized the *D* train was in the station loading passengers. In this haste to catch the train, he forcefully ran down the stairs, pushing aside three other people also going down the stairs. Mr. Parker, one of the three people, lost his footing and fell to the bottom of the stairs. Working on the platform, I saw Mr. Parker lose his footing as a result of Mr. Warren's actions, and I immediately went to his aid. Assistant Station Supervisor Brown was attracted to the incident after a crowd had gathered. After 15 minutes, the injured man, Mr. Parker, got up and boarded a train that was in the station and, therefore, he was not hurt seriously.

R. Sands #3214
Conductor

17. Since accident reports should only contain facts, which of the following should NOT be put into the accident report?
    A. The incident took place at the 34th Street Station.
    B. Mr. Parker was not hurt seriously.
    C. The date that the report was written
    D. Mr. Sands went to the aid of the injured an

6 (#1)

18. The title of the person submitting the report was   18._____
    A. Porter   B. Assistant Station Supervisor
    C. Conductor   D. Passenger

19. The TOTAL number of different persons mentioned in this report is   19._____
    A. seven   B. six   C. five   D. four

Questions 20-24.

DIRECTIONS: Questions 20 through 24 are to be answered SOLELY on the basis of the following report which is similar to those used in departments for reporting accidents,

REPORT OF ACCIDENT

Date of Accident 3/21   Tim: 3:43 P.M.   Date of Report: 3/24

<u>Department Vehicle</u>
Operator's Name: James Doe
Title: Motor Vehicle Operator
Vehicle Code No. 22-187
License Plate No.: 3N-1234

Damage to Vehicle: Right rear fender ripped, hubcap dented, rear bumper twisted
Place of Accident: 8th Avenue & 48th Street

<u>Vehicle No. 2</u>
Operator's Name: Richard Roe
Operator's Address: 841 W. 68th St.
Owner' Name: Jane Roe
Owner's Address: 2792 Beal Ave.
License Plate No. 8Y-6789
Damage to Vehicle: Grill, radiator, right side of front bumper, right-front fender and headlight crushed.

Description of Accident: I was driving east on 48th Street with the green light. I was almost across 8th Avenue when Ford panel truck started forth and crashed into my rear right fender. Denver of Ford used abusive language and accused me of rolling into his truck.

Persons Injured

Name <u>Richard Roe</u>   Address <u>841 W. 68TH Street</u>
Name _____   Address _____
Name _____   Address _____

20. Witnesses

Name <u>Richard Roe</u>   Address <u>841 W. 68th Street</u>
Name <u>John Brown</u>   Address <u>226 South Avenue</u>
Name <u>Mary Green</u>   Address <u>42 East Street</u>

<u>Report Prepared By James Doe</u>
Title <u>MVO</u> Badge No. <u>11346</u>

20. According to the above description of the accident, the diagram that would BEST show how and where the vehicles crashed is

A.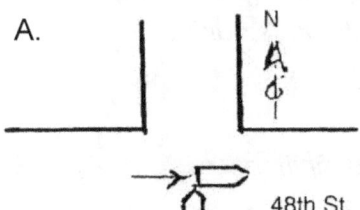
B.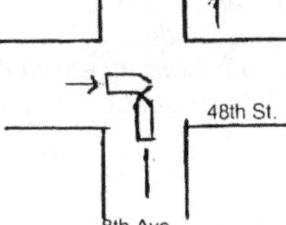
C.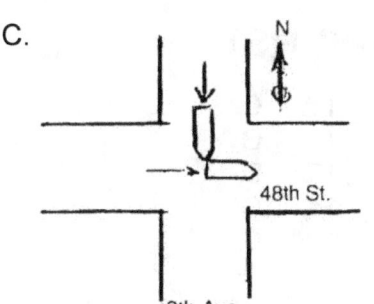
D.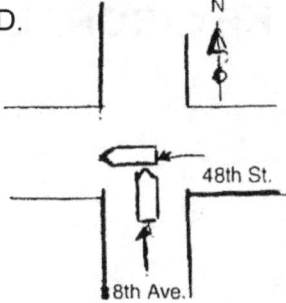

21. Of the following words used in the report, the one spelled INCORRECTLY is
 A. abussive B. accused C. radiator D. twisted

22. The city vehicle involved in this accident can BEST be identified
 A. as a panel truck
 B. the Department vehicle
 C. by the Badge Number of the operator
 D. by the Vehicle Code Number

23. According to the information in the report, the right-of-way belonged to
 A. neither vehicle B. the Department vehicle
 C. the vehicle that took it D. Vehicle No. 2

24. An entry on the report that seems to be INCORRECT is the
 A. first witness B. second witness
 C. third witness D. owner's name

25. Assume that the following passage is taken from a report which you, a deputy chief, receive from a battalion chief under your command. The report relates to a fire for which the department received public criticism because of delay in response and extension of fire to neighboring buildings. *Alarm from box ____ was received at 5:13 P.M. on Friday, October 2. All first alarm companies departed from quarters expeditiously but progress along the vehicle-glutted arterial thoroughfare was agonizingly slow. By dint of*

extraordinary effort and by virtue of great skill in maneuvering through impassable traffic, Engine Co. _____ arrived at the scene at 5:21 P.M. The sight which greeted them was a virtual Dante's INFERNO, of holocaust proportions. The hub of the conflagration was the penultimate structure of a row of houses, with extension impending to contiguous edifices.

The MAIN fault with the above report is that it
  A. contains spelling and punctuation errors
  B. contains unnecessary details
  C. uses words not in accordance with dictionary definitions
  D. uses inappropriate language and style.

KEY (CORRECT ANSWERS)

1.	B		11.	C
2.	D		12.	C
3.	A		13.	D
4.	C		14.	C
5.	B		15.	C
6.	B		16.	C
7.	D		17.	B
8.	B		18.	C
9.	A		19.	B
10.	C		20.	A

21.	A
22.	D
23.	B
24.	A
25.	D

TEST 2

DIRECTIONS: Each question or incomplete statement is followed by several suggested answers or completions. Select the one that BEST answers the question or completes the statement. *PRINT THE LETTER OF THE CORRECT ANSWER IN THE SPACE AT THE RIGHT.*

Questions 1-4.

DIRECTIONS: Questions 1 through 4 are to be answered on the basis of the information in the report below.

On February 15, Mr. Smith and Mr. Brown were injured in an accident occurring in the shop at 10 Long Road. No one was in the area of the accident other than Mr. Smith and Mr. Brown. Both of these employees described the following circumstances.

1. Mr. Brown saw the largest tool on the wall begin to fall from where it was hanging and run up to push Mr. Smith out of the way and to prevent the tool from falling, if possible.
2. Mr. Smith was standing near the wall under some tools which were hanging on nails in the wall.
3. Mr. Brown was standing a few steps from the wall.
4. Mr. Brown stepped toward Mr. Smith, who was on the floor and away from the falling tool. He tripped and fell over a piece of equipment on the floor.
5. Mr. Brown pushed Mr. Smith, who slipped on some grease on the floor and fell to the side, out of the way of the falling tool.
6. Mr. Brown tried to avoid Mr. Smith as he fell. In so doing, he fell against some pipes which were leaning against the wall. The pipes fell on both Mr. Brown and Mr. Smith.

Mr. Smith and Mr. Brown were both badly bruised and shaken. They were sent to the General Hospital to determine if any bones were broken. The office was later notified that neither employee was seriously hurt.

Since the accident, matters relating to safety and accident prevention around the shop have occupied the staff. There have been a number of complaints about the location of tools and equipment. Several employees are reluctant to work in the shop unless conditions are improved. Please advise as to the best way to handle this situation.

1. The one of the following which it is MOST important to add to the above memorandum is
    A. a signature line
    B. a transmittal note
    C. the date of the memo
    D. the initials of the typist

    1._____

2. The MOST logical order in which to list the circumstances relative to the accident is
    A. as shown (1, 2, 3, 4, 5, 6)
    B. 2, 3, 1, 5, 4, 6
    C. 1, 5, 4, 6, 3, 2
    D. 3, 2, 4, 6, 1, 5

    2._____

3. The one of the following which does NOT properly belong with the rest of the memorandum is
   A. the first section of paragraph 1
   B. the list of circumstances
   C. paragraph 2
   D. paragraph 3

4. According to the information in the memorandum, the BEST description of the subject is:
   A. Effect of accident on work output of the division
   B. Description of accident involving Mr. Smith and Mr. Brown
   C. Recommendations on how to avoid future accidents
   D. Safety and accident control in the shop

Questions 5-10.

DIRECTIONS: A ferry terminal supervisor is asked to write a report on the incident described in the following passage. Questions 5 through 10 are to be answered on the basis of the incident and the supervisor's report. Your answers should be based on the assumption that everything described in the passage is true.

On July 27, a rainy, foggy day, Joseph Jones and Steven Smith were in the Whitehall Ferry Terminal at about 9:50 A.M. waiting for the 10:00 A.M. ferry to Staten Island. Smith, seated with his legs stretched out in the aisle, was reading the sports page of the DAILY NEWS. Jones was walking by, drinking ginger ale from a cup. Neither man paid any attention to the other until Jones tripped over Smith's foot, fell to the floor, and dropped his drink. Smith looked at Jones as he lay on the floor and burst out laughing. Jones, infuriated, got up and punched Smith in the jaw. The force of the blow drove Smith's head back against the bench on which he was sitting. Smith did not fight back; he appeared to be dazed. Bystanders called a terminal worker, who assisted in making Smith as comfortable as possible.

One of the other people in the terminal for the ferry was a nurse, who examined Smith and told the ferry terminal supervisor that Smith probably had a concussion. An ambulance was called to take Smith to the hospital. A policeman arrived on the scene.

Jones' injury consisted of a sprained ankle and some bruises, but he refused medical attention. Jones explained to the supervisor what had happened. Jones truly regretted what he had done and went to the local police station with the policeman.

5. Of the following facts about the above incident, which one would be MOST important to include in the ferry terminal supervisor's report?
   A. The time the next boat was due to arrive
   B. Jones was carrying a cup of ginger ale
   C. Smith was sitting with his legs stretched out in the aisle
   D. Why Smith and Jones were in the terminal

6. The MAIN purpose of writing a report of the above incident is to
   A. make recommendations for preventing fights in the terminal
   B. state the important facts of the incident
   C. blame Jones for not looking where he was going
   D. provide evidence that Smith was not at fault

7. An adequate report of the above incident MUST give the names of the participants, the names of witnesses, and the
    A. date, the place, the time, and the events that took place
    B. date, the events that took place, the time, and the names of the terminal personnel on duty that day
    C. place, the names of the terminal personnel on duty that day, the weather conditions, and the events which took place
    D. names of the passengers in the terminal, the time, the place, and the events which took place

8. The supervisor asked for individuals who had witnessed the entire incident to give their account of what they had seen. Thomas White, a twelve-year-old boy said that Jones fell, got up, turned, and then hit Smith.
Thomas White's description of the incident is
    A. *adequate*; it is truthful, straight-forward, and includes necessary details
    B. *adequate;* it shows that the incident was not started on purpose
    C. *inadequate*; he is too young to understand the implications of his testimony
    D. *inadequate*; it omits certain pertinent facts about the incident

9. Another witness, Mary Collins, told the ferry terminal supervisor that when she heard Jones fall, she looked in that direction and saw Jones get up and hit Smith, who was laughing. She immediately ran to find a terminal worker to prevent further fighting. When she returned, she found Smith slumped on the bench.
Mrs. Collins' report is USEFUL because
    A. it proves that Smith antagonized Jones
    B. it indicates that Jones beat Smith repeatedly
    C. she witnessed that Jones hit Smith
    D. it shows that only one punch was thrown

10. Based on the description given above, which of the following would be the MOST accurate summary for the ferry terminal supervisor to put in his report?
    A. Jones fell and Smith laughed, which caused Jones to beat him until bystanders got a terminal worker to separate them.
    B. Smith was reading a newspaper when Jones fell. Then Jones hit Smith and dazed him. Smith was examined by a nurse who said that Smith had a serious concussion.
    C. Jones tripped accidentally over Smith's legs and fell. Smith laughed at Jones, who lost his temper and hit Smith, driving Smith's head against the back of a bench.
    D. Smith antagonized Jones first, by tripping him second, by laughing at him, and third by not fighting back. Smith was aided by a nurse and went to the hospital.

Questions 11-13.

DIRECTIONS: Questions 11 through 13 are to be answered SOLELY on the basis of the following report.

To: John Greene
General Park Foreman

Date: May 5

From: Earl Jones
Gardener

Subject:

On May 3rd, as I was finishing a job six feet from the boat-house, I observed that the hole which had been filled in last week was now not level with the ground around it. This seems to be a hazardous condition because it might cause pedestrians to fall into it. I, therefore, suggest that this job be redone as soon as possible.

11. This report should be considered poorly written MAINLY because
    A. it does not give enough information to take appropriate action
    B. too many different tenses are used
    C. it describes no actual personal injury to anyone
    D. there is no recommendation in the report to remedy the situation

12. It is noted that the subject of the report has been left out.
    Which of the following statements would be BEST as the subject of this report?
    A. Observation made by Earl Jones, Gardener
    B. Deteriorating condition of park grounds
    C. Report of dangerous condition near boathouse
    D. A dangerous walk through the park

13. In order for John Greene to take appropriate action, additional information should be added to the report giving the
    A. exact date the repair was made
    B. exact location of the hole
    C. exact time the observation was made
    D. names of the crew who previously filled in the hole

Questions 14-18.

DIRECTIONS: Questions 14 through 18 consist of sets of four sentences lettered A, B, C, and D. For each question, choose the sentence which is grammatically and stylistically MOST appropriate for use in a formal written report.

14. A. It is recommended, therefore, that the impasse panel hearings are to be convened on September 30.
    B. It is therefore recommended that the impasse panel hearings be convened on September 30.
    C. Therefore, it is recommended to convene the impasse panel hearings on September 30.
    D. It is recommended that the impasse panel hearings therefore should be convened on September 30.

15.
  A. Penalties have been assessed for violating the Taylor Law by several unions.
  B. When they violated provisions of the Taylor Law, several unions were later penalized.
  C. Several unions have been penalized for violating provisions of the Taylor Law.
  D. Several unions' violating provisions of the Taylor Law resulted in them being penalized.

15._____

16.
  A. The number of disputes settled through mediation has increased significantly over the past two years.
  B. The number of disputes settled through mediation are increasing significantly over two-year periods.
  C. Over the past two years, through mediation, the number of disputes settled increased significantly.
  D. There is a significant increase over the past two years of the number of disputes settled through mediation.

16._____

17.
  A. The union members will vote to determine if the contract is to be approved.
  B. It is not yet known whether the union members will ratify the proposed contract.
  C. When the union members vote, that will determine the new contract.
  D. Whether the union members will ratify the proposed contract, it is not yet known.

17._____

18.
  A. The parties agreed to an increase in fringe benefits in return for greater worker productivity.
  B. Greater productivity was agreed to be provided in return for increased fringe benefits.
  C. Productivity and fringe benefits are interrelated; the higher the former, the more the latter grows.
  D. The contract now provides that the amount of fringe benefits will depend upon the level of output by the workers.

18._____

19. Of the following excerpts, selected from letters, the one which is considered by modern letter writing experts to be the BEST is:
  A. Attached please find the application form to be filled out by you. Return the form to this office at the above address.
  B. Forward to this office your check accompanied by the application form enclosed with this letter.
  C. If you wish to apply, please complete and return the enclosed form with your check.
  D. In reply to your letter of December _____, enclosed herewith please find the application form you requested.

19._____

20. A city employee who writes a letter requesting information from a businessman should realize that, of the following, it is MOST important to
    A. end the letter with a polite closing
    B. make the letter short enough to fit on one page
    C. use a form, such as a questionnaire, to save the businessman's time
    D. use a courteous tone that will get the desired cooperation

Questions 21-22.

DIRECTIONS: Questions 21 and 22 consist of four sentences. Choose the one sentence in each set of four that would be BEST for a formal letter or report. Consider grammar and appropriate usage.

21. A. Most all the work he completed before he become ill.
    B. He completed most of the work before becoming ill.
    C. Prior to him becoming ill, his work was mostly completed.
    D. Before he became ill most of the work he had completed.

22. A. Being that the report lacked a clearly worded recommendation, it did not matter that it contained enough information.
    B. There was enough information in the report, although it, including the recommendation, were not clearly worded.
    C. Although the report contained enough information, it did not have a clearly worded recommendation.
    D. Though the report did not have a recommendation that was clearly worded, and the information therein contained was enough.

Questions 23-25.

DIRECTIONS: In Questions 23 through 25, choose the sentence which is BEST from the point of view of English usage suitable for a business letter or report.

23. A. Answering of veterans' inquiries, together with the receipt of fees, have been handled by the Bursar's Office since the new President came.
    B. Since the new President's arrival, the handling of all veteran's inquiries has been turned over to the Bursar's Office.
    C. In addition to the receipt of fees, the Bursar's Office has been handling veterans' inquiries since the new President came.
    D. The principle change in the work of the Bursar's Office since the new President came is that it now handles veterans' inquiries as well as the receipt of fees.

24. A. The current unrest about education undoubtedly stems in part from the fact that the people fear the basic purposes of the schools are being neglected or supplanted by spurious ones.
    B. The fears of people that the basic purposes of the schools are being neglected or supplanted by spurious ones contributes to the current unrest about education.

C. Undoubtedly some responsibility for the current unrest about education must be assigned to peoples' fears that the purpose and base of the school system is being neglected or supplanted.
D. From the fears of people that the basic purposes of the schools are being neglected or supplanted by spurious ones undoubtedly stem in part the current unrest about education.

25.
A. The existence of administrative phenomena are clearly established, but their characteristics, relations and laws are obscure.
B. The obscurity of the characteristics, relations and laws of administrative phenomena do not preclude their existence.
C. Administrative phenomena clearly exists in spite of the obscurity of their characteristics, relations and laws.
D. The characteristics, relations and laws of administrative phenomena are obscure but the existence of the phenomena is clear.

25.____

KEY (CORRECT ANSWERS)

1.	C		11.	A
2.	B		12.	C
3.	D		13.	B
4.	B		14.	B
5.	C		15.	C
6.	B		16.	A
7.	A		17.	B
8.	D		18.	A
9.	C		19.	C
10.	C		20.	D

21. B
22. C
23. C
24. A
25. D

TEST 3

DIRECTIONS: Each question or incomplete statement is followed by several suggested answers or completions. Select the one that BEST answers the question or completes the statement. *PRINT THE LETTER OF THE CORRECT ANSWER IN THE SPACE AT THE RIGHT.*

1. Of the following, the BEST statement concerning the placement of *Conclusions and Recommendations* in a management report is:
   A. Recommendations should always be included in a report unless the report presents the results of an investigation.
   B. If a report presents conclusions, it must present recommendations.
   C. Every statement that is a conclusion should grow out of facts given elsewhere in the report.
   D. Conclusions and recommendations should always conclude the report because they depend on its contents.

   1.____

2. Assume you are preparing a systematic analysis of our agency's pest control program and its effect on eliminating rodent infestation of premises in a specific region. To omit from your report important facts which you originally received from the person to whom you are recording is GENERALLY considered to be
   A. *desirable*; anyone who is likely to read the report can consult his files for extra information
   B. *undesirable*; the report should include major facts that are obtained as a result of your efforts
   C. *desirable*; the person you are reporting to does not pass the report on to others who lack his own familiarity with the subject
   D. *undesirable*; the report should include all of the facts that are obtained as a result of your efforts

   2.____

3. Of all the non-verbal devices used in report writing, tables are used most frequently to enable a reader to compare statistical information more easily. Hence, it is important that an analyst know when to use tables.
   Which one of the following statements that relate to tables is generally considered to be LEAST valid?
   A. A table from an outside source must be acknowledged by the report writer.
   B. A table should be placed far in advance of the point where it is referred to or discussed in the report.
   C. The notes applying to a table are placed at the bottom of the table, rather than at the bottom of the page on which the table is found.
   D. A table should indicate the major factors that effect the data it contains.

   3.____

4. Assume that an analyst writes reports which contain more detail than might be needed to serve their purpose. Such a practice is GENERALLY considered to be
   A. *desirable*; this additional detail permits maximized machine utilization
   B. *undesirable*; if specifications of reports are defined when they are first set up, loss of flexibility will follow

   4.____

C. *desirable*; everything ought to be recorded so it will be there if it is ever needed
D. *undesirable*; recipients of these reports are likely to discredit them entirely

Questions 5-6.

DIRECTIONS: Questions 5 and 6 consist of sentences lettered A, B, C, and D. For each question, choose the sentence which is stylistically and grammatically MOST appropriate for a management report.

5. A. For too long, the citizen has been forced to rely for his productivity information on the whims, impressions, and uninformed opinion of public spokesmen.
   B. For too long, the citizen has been forced to base his information about productivity on the whims, impressions and uninformed opinion of public spokesmen.
   C. The citizen has been forced do base his information about productivity on the whims, impressions and uninformed opinion of public spokesmen for too long.
   D. The citizen has been forced for too long to rely for his productivity information on the whims, impressions and uninformed opinion of public spokesmen.

5._____

6. A. More competition means lower costs to the city, thereby helping to compensate for inflation.
   B. More competition, helping to compensate for inflation, means lower costs to the city.
   C. Inflation may be compensated for by more competition, which will reduce the city's costs.
   D. The costs to the city will be lessened by more competition, helping to compensate for inflation.

6._____

Questions 7-11.

DIRECTIONS: In Questions 7 through 11, choose the sentence which is BEST from the point of view of English usage suitable for a business letter or report.

7. A. It is the opinion of the Commissioners that programs which include the construction of cut-rate municipal garages in the central business district is inadvisable.
   B. Having reviewed the material submitted, the program for putting up cut-rate garages in the central business district seemed likely to cause traffic congestion.
   C. The Commissioners believe that putting up cut-rate municipal garages in the central business district is inadvisable.
   D. Making an effort to facilitate the cleaning of streets in the central business district, the building of cut-rate municipal garages presents the problem that it would encourage more motorists to come into the central city.

7._____

8. A. This letter, together with the reports, are to be sent to the principal.
    B. The reports, together with this letter, is to be sent to the principal.
    C. The reports and this letter is to be sent to the principal.
    D. This letter, together with the reports, is to be sent to the principal.

9. A. Each employee has to decide for themselves whether to take the examination.
    B. Each of the employees has to decide or himself whether to take the examination.
    C. Each of the employees has to decide for themselves whether to take the examination.
    D. Each of the employees have to decide for himself whether to take the examination.

10. A. The reason a new schedule is being prepared is that there has been a change in priorities.
    B. Because there has been a change in priorities is the reason why a new schedule is being made up.
    C. The reason why a new schedule is being made up is because there been a change in priorities.
    D. Because of a change in priorities is the reason why a new schedule is being prepared.

11. A. The changes in procedure had an unfavorable affect upon the output of the unit.
    B. The increased output of the unit was largely due to the affect of the procedural changes.
    C. The changes in procedure had the effect of increasing the output of the unit.
    D. The increased output of the unit from the procedural changes were the effect.

Questions 12-19.

DIRECTIONS: Questions 12 through 19 each consist of four sentences. Choose the one sentence in each set of four that would be BEST for a formal letter or report. Consider grammar and appropriate usage.

12. A. These statements can be depended on, for their truth has been guaranteed by reliable employees.
    B. Reliable city employees guarantee the facts with regards to the truth of these statements.
    C. Most all these statements have been supported by city employees who are reliable and can be depended upon.
    D. The city employees which have guaranteed these statements are reliable.

13. A. I believe the letter was addressed to either my associate or I.
    B. If properly addressed, the letter will reach my associate and I.
    C. My associate's name, as well as mine, was on the letter.
    D. The letter had been addressed to myself and my associate.

14. A. The secretary would have corrected the errors if she knew that the supervisor would see the report.
    B. The supervisor reprimanded the secretary, whom she believed had made careless errors.
    C. Many errors were found in the report which she typed and could not disregard.
    D. The errors in the typed report were so numerous that they could hardly be overlooked.

15. A. His consultant was as pleased as he with the success of the project.
    B. The success of the project pleased both his consultant and he.
    C. He and also his consultant was pleased with the success of the project.
    D. Both his consultant and he was pleased with the success of the project.

16. A. Since the letter did not contain the needed information, he could not use it.
    B. Being that the letter lacked the needed information, he could not use it.
    C. Since the letter lacked the needed information, it was of no use to him.
    D. This letter was useless to him because there was no needed information in it.

17. A. Scarcely had the real estate tax increase been declared than the notices were sent out.
    B. They had no sooner declared the real estate tax increases when they sent the notices to the owners.
    C. The city had hardly declared the real estate tax increase till the notices were prepared for mailing.
    D. No sooner had the real estate tax increase been declared than the notices were sent out

18. A. Though deeply effected by the setback, the advice given by the admissions office began to seem more reasonable.
    B. Although he was deeply effected by the setback, the advice given by the admissions office began to seem more reasonable.
    C. Though the setback had affected him deeply, the advise given by the admissions office began to see more reasonable.
    D. Although he was deeply affected by the setback, the advice given by the admissions office began to seem more reasonable.

19. A. Returning to the administration building after attendance at a meeting, the door was locked despite an agreement that it would be left open.
    B. When he returned to the administration building after attending a meeting, he found the door locked, despite an agreement that it would be left open.
    C. After attending a meeting, the door to the administration building was locked, despite an agreement that it would be left open.
    D. When he returned to the administration building after attendance at a meeting, he found the door locked, despite an agreement that it would be left open.

20. A. A formal business report may consist of many parts, including the following:
    1. Table of Contents
    2. List of references
    3. Preface
    4. Index
    5. List of Tables
    6. Conclusions or recommendations

    Of the following, in setting up a formal report, the PROPER order of the six parts listed is:
    A. 1, 3, 6, 5, 2, 4
    B. 4, 3, 2, 5, 6 1
    C. 3, 1, 5, 6, 2, 4
    D. 2, 5, 3, 1, 4, 6

21. Suppose you are writing a report on an interview you have just completed with a particularly hostile applicant for public assistance.
    Which of the following BEST describes what you should include in this report?
    A. What you think caused the applicant's hostile attitude during the interview
    B. Specific examples of the applicant's hostile remarks and behavior
    C. The relevant information uncovered during the interview
    D. A recommendation that the applicant's request be denied because of his hostility.

22. When including recommendations in a report to your supervisor, which of the following is MOST important for you to do?
    A. Provide several alternative courses of action for each recommendation.
    B. First present the supporting evidence, then the recommendations.
    C. First present the recommendations, then the supporting evidence.
    D. Make sure the recommendations arise logically out of the information in the report.

23. It is often necessary that the writer of a report present facts and sufficient arguments to gain acceptance of the points, conclusions, or recommendations set forth in the report.
    Of the following, the LEAST advisable step to take in organizing a report, when such argumentation is the important factor, is a(n)
    A. elaborate expression of personal belief
    B. businesslike discussion of the problem as a whole
    C, orderly arrangement of convincing data
    D. reasonable explanation of the primary issues

24. Assume that a clerk is asked to prepare a special report which he has not prepared before. He decides to make a written outline of the report before writing it in full. This decision by the clerk is
    A. *good*, mainly because it helps the writer to organize his thoughts and decide what will go into the report
    B. *good*, mainly because it clearly shows the number of topics, number of '

C. *poor*, mainly because it wastes the time of the writer since he will have to write the full report anyway.
D. *poor*, mainly because it confines the writer to those areas listed in the outline

25. Assume that a clerk in the water resources central shop is asked to prepare an important report, giving the location and condition of various fire hydrants in the city. One of the hydrants in question is broken and is spewing rusty water in the street, creating a flooded condition in the area. The clerk reports that the hydrant is broken but does not report the escaping water or the flood.
Of the following, the BEST evaluation of the clerk's decision about what to report is that it is basically
    A. *correct*; chiefly because a lengthy report would contain irrelevant information
    B. *correct*; chiefly because a more detailed description of a hydrant should be made by a fireman, not a clerk
    C. *incorrect*; chiefly because the clerk's assignment was to describe the condition of the hydrant and he should give a full explanation
    D. *incorrect*; chiefly because the clerk should include as much information as possible in his report whether or not it is relevant

25._____

KEY (CORRECT ANSWERS)

1.	C		11.	C
2.	B		12.	A
3.	B		13.	C
4.	D		14.	D
5.	B		15.	A
6.	A		16.	C
7.	C		17.	D
8.	D		18.	D
9.	B		19.	B
10.	A		20.	C

21.	C
22.	D
23.	A
24.	A
25.	C

READING COMPREHENSION
UNDERSTANDING AND INTERPRETING WRITTEN MATERIAL
EXAMINATION SECTION
TEST 1

DIRECTIONS: Each question or incomplete statement is followed by several suggested answers or completions. Select the one that BEST answers the question or completes the statement. *PRINT THE LETTER OF THE CORRECT ANSWER IN THE SPACE AT THE RIGHT.*

Questions 1-8.

DIRECTIONS: Questions 1 through 8 are to be answered on the basis of the following regulations governing Newspaper Carriers when on subway trains or station platforms. These Newspaper Carriers are issued badges which entitle them to enter subway stations, when carrying papers in accordance with these regulations, without paying a fare.

REGULATIONS GOVERNING NEWSPAPER CARRIERS WHEN ON SUBWAY TRAINS OR STATION PLATFORMS

1. Carriers must wear badges at all times when on trains.
2. Carriers must not sort, separate, or wrap bundles on trains or insert sections.
3. Carriers must not obstruct platform of cars or stations.
4. Carriers may make delivery to stands inside the stations by depositing their badge with the station agent.
5. Throwing of bundles is strictly prohibited and will be cause for arrest.
6. Each bundle must not be over 18" x 12" x 15".
7. Not more than two bundles shall be carried by each carrier. (An extra fare to be charged for a second bundle.)
8. No wire to be used on bundles carried into stations.

1. These regulations do NOT prohibit carriers on trains from _____ newspapers. 1._____

   A. sorting bundles of
   B. carrying bundles of
   C. wrapping bundles of
   D. inserting sections into

2. A carrier delivering newspapers to a stand inside of the station MUST 2._____

   A. wear his badge at all times
   B. leave his badge with the railroad clerk
   C. show his badge to the railroad clerk
   D. show his badge at the newsstand

3. Carriers are warned against throwing bundles of newspapers from trains MAINLY because these acts may 3._____

   A. wreck the stand
   B. cause injury to passengers
   C. hurt the carrier
   D. damage the newspaper

117

4. It is permissible for a carrier to temporarily leave his bundles of newspapers

   A. near the subway car's door
   B. at the foot of the station stairs
   C. in front of the exit gate
   D. on a station bench

5. Of the following, the carrier who should NOT be restricted from entering the subway is the one carrying a bundle which is _____ long, _____ wide, and _____ high.

   A. 15"; 18"; 18"
   B. 18"; 12"; 18"
   C. 18"; 12"; 15"
   D. 18"; 15"; 15"

6. A carrier who will have to pay one fare is carrying _____ bundle(s).

   A. one
   B. two
   C. three
   D. four

7. Wire may NOT be used for tying bundles because it may be

   A. rusty
   B. expensive
   C. needed for other purposes
   D. dangerous to other passengers

8. If a carrier is arrested in violation of these regulations, the PROBABLE reason is that he

   A. carried too many papers
   B. was not wearing his badge
   C. separated bundles of newspapers on the train
   D. tossed a bundle of newspapers to a carrier on a train

Questions 9-12.

DIRECTIONS: Questions 9 through 12 are to be answered on the basis of the Bulletin printed below. Read this Bulletin carefully before answering these questions. Select your answers ONLY on the basis of this Bulletin.

BULLETIN

Rule 107(m) states, in part, that *Before closing doors they (Conductors) must afford passengers an opportunity to detrain and entrain...*

Doors must be left open long enough to allow passengers to enter and exit from the train. Closing doors on passengers too quickly does not help to shorten the station stop and is a violation of the safety and courtesy which must be accorded to all our passengers.

The proper and effective way to keep passengers moving in and out of the train is to use the public address system. When the train is excessively crowded and passengers on the platform are pushing those in the cars, it may be necessary to close the doors after a reasonable period of time has been allowed.

Closing doors on passengers too quickly is a violation of rules and will be cause for disciplinary actions.

9. Which of the following statements is CORRECT about closing doors on passengers too quickly? It

   A. will shorten the running time from terminal to terminal
   B. shortens the station stop but is a violation of safety and courtesy
   C. does not help shorten the station stop time
   D. makes the passengers detrain and entrain quicker

10. The BEST way to get passengers to move in and out of cars quickly is to

    A. have the platform conductors urge passengers to move into doorways
    B. make announcements over the public address system
    C. start closing doors while passengers are getting on
    D. set a fixed time for stopping at each station

11. The conductor should leave doors open at each station stop long enough for passengers to

    A. squeeze into an excessively crowded train
    B. get from the local to the express train
    C. get off and get on the train
    D. hear the announcements over the public address system

12. Closing doors on passengers too quickly is a violation of rules and is cause for

    A. the conductor's immediate suspension
    B. the conductor to be sent back to the terminal for another assignment
    C. removal of the conductor at the next station
    D. disciplinary action to be taken against the conductor

Questions 13-15.

DIRECTIONS: Questions 13 through 15 are to be answered on the basis of the Bulletin printed below. Read this Bulletin carefully before answering these questions. Select your answers ONLY on the basis of this Bulletin.

BULLETIN

Conductors assigned to train service are not required to wear uniform caps from June 1 to September 30, inclusive.

Conductors assigned to platform duty are required to wear the uniform cap at all times. Conductors are reminded that they must furnish their badge numbers to anyone who requests same.

During the above-mentioned period, conductors may remove their uniform coats. The regulation summer short-sleeved shirts must be worn with the regulation uniform trousers. Suspenders are not permitted if the uniform coat is removed. Shoes are to be black but sandals, sneakers, suede, canvas, or two-tone footwear must not be worn.

Conductors may work without uniform tie if the uniform coat is removed. However, only the top collar button may be opened. The tie may not be removed if the uniform coat is worn.

13. Conductors assigned to platform duty are required to wear uniform caps

    A. at all times except from June 1 to September 30, inclusive
    B. whenever they are on duty
    C. only from June 1 to September 30, inclusive
    D. only when they remove their uniform coats

14. Suspenders are permitted ONLY if conductors wear

    A. summer short-sleeved shirts with uniform trousers
    B. uniform trousers without belt loops
    C. the type permitted by the authority
    D. uniform coats

15. A conductor MUST furnish his badge number to

    A. authority supervisors only
    B. members of special inspection only
    C. anyone who asks him for it
    D. passengers only

Questions 16-17.

DIRECTIONS: Questions 16 and 17 are to be answered SOLELY on the basis of the following Bulletin.

BULLETIN

Effective immediately, Conductors on trains equipped with public address systems shall make the following announcements in addition to their regular station announcement. At stations where passengers normally board trains from their homes or places of employment, the announcement shall be *Good Morning* or *Good Afternoon* or *Good Evening,* depending on the time of the day. At stations where passengers normally leave trains for their homes or places of employment, the announcement shall be *Have a Good Day* or *Good Night,* depending on the time of day or night.

16. The MAIN purpose of making the additional announcements mentioned in the Bulletin is MOST likely to

    A. keep passengers informed about the time of day
    B. determine whether the public address system works in case of an emergency
    C. make the passengers' ride more pleasant
    D. have the conductor get used to using the public address system

17. According to this Bulletin, a conductor should greet passengers boarding the *D* train at the Coney Island Station at 8 A.M. Monday by announcing

    A. Have a Good Day
    B. Good Morning
    C. Watch your step as you leave
    D. Good Evening

Questions 18-25.

DIRECTIONS: Questions 18 through 25 are to be answered on the basis of the information regarding the incident given below. Read this information carefully before answering these questions.

INCIDENT

As John Brown, a cleaner, was sweeping the subway station platform, in accordance with his assigned schedule, he was accused by Henry Adams of unnecessarily bumping him with the broom and scolded for doing this work when so many passengers were on the platform. Adams obtained Brown's badge number and stated that he would report the matter to the Transit Authority. Standing around and watching this were Mary Smith, a schoolteacher, Ann Jones, a student, and Joe Black, a maintainer, with Jim Roe, his helper, who had been working on one of the turnstiles. Brown thereupon proceeded to take the names and addresses of these people as required by the Transit Authority rule which directs that names and addresses of as many disinterested witnesses be taken as possible. Shortly thereafter, a train arrived at the station and Adams, as well as several other people, boarded the train and left. Brown went back to his work of sweeping the station.

18. The cleaner was sweeping the station at this time because

    A. the platform was unusually dirty
    B. there were very few passengers on the platform
    C. he had no regard for the passengers
    D. it was set by his work schedule

19. This incident proves that

    A. witnesses are needed in such cases
    B. porters are generally careless
    C. subway employees stick together
    D. brooms are dangerous in the subway

20. Joe Black was a

    A. helper   B. maintainer
    C. cleaner   D. teacher

21. The number of persons witnessing this incident was

    A. 2   B. 3   C. 4   D. 5

22. The addresses of witnesses are required so that they may later be

    A. depended on to testify   B. recognized
    C. paid   D. located

23. The person who said he would report this incident to the transit authority was

    A. Black   B. Adams   C. Brown   D. Roe

24. The ONLY person of the following who positively did NOT board the train was 24.____

    A. Brown B. Smith C. Adams D. Jones

25. As a result of this incident, 25.____

    A. no action need be taken against the cleaner unless Adams makes a written complaint
    B. the cleaner should be given the rest of the day off
    C. the handles of the brooms used should be made shorter
    D. Brown's badge number should be changed

KEY (CORRECT ANSWERS)

1.	B	11.	C
2.	B	12.	D
3.	B	13.	B
4.	D	14.	D
5.	C	15.	C
6.	A	16.	C
7.	D	17.	B
8.	D	18.	D
9.	C	19.	A
10.	B	20.	B

21. C
22. D
23. B
24. A
25. A

TEST 2

DIRECTIONS: Each question or incomplete statement is followed by several suggested answers or completions. Select the one that BEST answers the question or completes the statement. *PRINT THE LETTER OF THE CORRECT ANSWER IN THE SPACE AT THE RIGHT.*

Questions 1-10.

DIRECTIONS: Questions 1 through 10 are to be answered on the basis of the information contained in the following safety rules. Read the rules carefully before answering these questions.

SAFETY RULES

Employees must take every precaution to prevent accidents, or injury to persons, or damage to property. For this reason, they must observe conditions of the equipment and tools with which they work, and the structures upon which they work.

It is the duty of all employees to report to their superior all dangerous conditions which they may observe. Employees must use every precaution to prevent the origin of fire. If they discover smoke or a fire in the subway, they shall proceed to the nearest telephone and notify the trainmaster giving their name, badge number, and location of the trouble.

In case of accidents on the subway system, employees must, if possible, secure the name, address, and telephone number of any passengers who may have been injured.

Employees at or near the location of trouble on the subway system, whether it be a fire or an accident, shall render all practical assistance which they are qualified to perform.

1. The BEST way for employees to prevent an accident is to 1.____
   A. secure the names of the injured persons
   B. arrive promptly at the location of the accident
   C. give their name and badge numbers to the trainmaster
   D. take all necessary precautions

2. In case of trouble, trackmen are NOT expected to 2.____
   A. report fires
   B. give help if they don't know how
   C. secure telephone numbers of persons injured in subway accidents
   D. give their badge number to anyone

3. Trackmen MUST 3.____
   A. be present at all fires
   B. see all accidents
   C. report dangerous conditions
   D. be the first to discover smoke in the subway

4. Observing conditions means to

   A. look at things carefully
   B. report what you see
   C. ignore things that are none of your business
   D. correct dangerous conditions

5. A dangerous condition existing on the subway system which a trackman should observe and report to his superior would be

   A. passengers crowding into trains
   B. trains running behind schedule
   C. tools in defective condition
   D. some newspapers on the track

6. If a trackman discovers a badly worn rail, he should

   A. not take any action
   B. remove the worn section of rail
   C. notify his superior
   D. replace the rail

7. The MAIN reason a trackman should observe the condition of his tools is

   A. so that they won't be stolen
   B. because they don't belong to him
   C. to prevent accidents
   D. because they cannot be replaced

8. If a passenger who paid his fare is injured in a subway accident, it is MOST important that an employee obtain the passenger's

   A. name
   B. age
   C. badge number
   D. destination

9. An employee who happens to be at the scene of an accident on a crowded station of the system should

   A. not give assistance unless he chooses to do so
   B. leave the scene immediately
   C. question all bystanders
   D. render whatever assistance he can

10. If a trackman discovers a fire at one end of a station platform and telephones the information to the trainmaster, he need NOT give

    A. the trainmaster's name
    B. the name of the station involved
    C. his own name
    D. the number of his badge

Questions 11-15.

DIRECTIONS: Questions 11 through 15 are to be answered on the basis of the information contained in the safety regulations given below. Refer to these rules in answering these questions.

REGULATIONS FOR SMALL GROUPS WHO MOVE FROM POINT TO POINT ON THE TRACKS

Employees who perform duties on the tracks in small groups and who move from point to point along the trainway must be on the alert at all times and prepared to clear the track when a train approaches without unnecessarily slowing it down. Underground at all times, and out-of-doors between sunset and sunrise, such employees must not enter upon the tracks unless each of them is equipped with an approved light. Flashlights must not be used for protection by such groups. Upon clearing the track to permit a train to pass, each member of the group must give a proceed signal, by hand or light, to the motorman of the train. Whenever such small groups are working in an area protected by caution lights or flags, but are not members of the gang for whom the flagging protection was established, they must not give proceed signals to motormen. The purpose of this rule is to avoid a motorman's confusing such signal with that of the flagman who is protecting a gang. Whenever a small group is engaged in work of an engrossing nature or at any time when the view of approaching trains is limited by reason of curves or otherwise, one man of the group, equipped with a whistle, must be assigned properly to warn and protect the man or men at work and must not perform any other duties while so assigned.

11. If a small group of men are traveling along the tracks toward their work location and a train approaches, they should

    A. stop the train
    B. signal the motorman to go slowly
    C. clear the track
    D. stop immediately

12. Small groups may enter upon the tracks

    A. only between sunset and sunrise
    B. provided each has an approved light
    C. provided their foreman has a good flashlight
    D. provided each man has an approved flashlight

13. After a small group has cleared the tracks in an area unprotected by caution lights or flags,

    A. each member must give the proceed signal to the motorman
    B. the foreman signals the motorman to proceed
    C. the motorman can proceed provided he goes slowly
    D. the last member off the tracks gives the signal to the motorman

14. If a small group is working in an area protected by the signals of a track gang, the members of the small group

    A. need not be concerned with train movement
    B. must give the proceed signal together with the track gang

C. can delegate one of their members to give the proceed signal
D. must not give the proceed signal

15. If the view of approaching trains is blocked, the small group should

    A. move to where they can see the trains
    B. delegate one of the group to warn and protect them
    C. keep their ears alert for approaching trains
    D. refuse to work at such locations

Questions 16-25.

DIRECTIONS: Questions 16 through 25 are to be answered SOLELY on the basis of the article about general safety precautions given below.

GENERAL SAFETY PRECAUTIONS

When work is being done on or next to a track on which regular trains are running, special signals must be displayed as called for in the general rules for flagging. Yellow caution signals, green clear signals, and a flagman with a red danger signal are required for the protection of traffic and workmen in accordance with the standard flagging rules. The flagman shall also carry a white signal for display to the motorman when he may proceed. The foreman in charge must see that proper signals are displayed.

On elevated lines during daylight hours, the yellow signal shall be a yellow flag, the red signal shall be a red flag, the green signal shall be a green flag, and the white signal shall be a white flag. In subway sections, and on elevated lines after dark, the yellow signal shall be a yellow lantern, the red signal shall be a red lantern, the green signal shall be a green lantern, and the white signal shall be a white lantern.

Caution and clear signals are to be secured to the elevated or subway structure with non-metallic fastenings outside the clearance line of the train and on the motorman's side of the track.

16. On elevated lines during daylight hours, the caution signal is a

    A. yellow lantern   B. green lantern
    C. yellow flag   D. green flag

17. In subway sections, the clear signal is a

    A. yellow lantern   B. green lantern
    C. yellow flag   D. green flag

18. The MINIMUM number of lanterns that a subway track flagman should carry is

    A. 1   B. 2   C. 3   D. 4

19. The PRIMARY purpose of flagging is to protect the

    A. flagman   B. motorman
    C. track workers   D. railroad

20. A suitable fastening for securing caution lights to the elevated or subway structure is   20.____

    A. copper nails   B. steel wire
    C. brass rods   D. cotton twine

21. On elevated structures during daylight hours, the red flag is held by the   21.____

    A. motorman   B. foreman   C. trackman   D. flagman

22. The signal used in the subway to notify a motorman to proceed is a   22.____

    A. white lantern   B. green lantern
    C. red flag   D. yellow flag

23. The caution, clear, and danger signals are displayed for the information of   23.____

    A. trackmen   B. workmen   C. flagmen   D. motormen

24. Since the motorman's cab is on the right-hand side, caution signals should be secured to the   24.____

    A. right-hand running rail
    B. left-hand running rail
    C. structure to the right of the track
    D. structure to the left of the track

25. In a track work gang, the person responsible for the proper display of signals is the   25.____

    A. track worker   B. foreman
    C. motorman   D. flagman

KEY (CORRECT ANSWERS)

1. D
2. B
3. C
4. A
5. C
6. C
7. C
8. A
9. D
10. A
11. C
12. B
13. A
14. D
15. B
16. C
17. B
18. B
19. C
20. D
21. D
22. A
23. D
24. C
25. B

TEST 3

DIRECTIONS: Each question or incomplete statement is followed by several suggested answers or completions. Select the one that BEST answers the question or completes the statement. *PRINT THE LETTER OF THE CORRECT ANSWER IN THE SPACE AT THE RIGHT.*

Questions 1-6.

DIRECTIONS: Questions 1 through 6 are to be answered on the basis of the Bulletin Order given below. Refer to this bulletin when answering these questions.

BULLETIN ORDER NO. 67

SUBJECT: Procedure for Handling Fire Occurrences

In order that the Fire Department may be notified of all fires, even those that have been extinguished by our own employees, any employee having knowledge of a fire must notify the Station Department Office immediately on telephone extensions D-4177, D-4181, D-4185, or D-4189.

Specific information regarding the fire should include the location of the fire, the approximate distance north or south of the nearest station, and the track designation, line, and division.

In addition, the report should contain information as to the status of the fire and whether our forces have extinguished it or if Fire Department equipment is required.

When all information has been obtained, the Station Supervisor in Charge in the Station Department Office will notify the Desk Trainmaster of the Division involved.

Richard Roe,
Superintendent

1. An employee having knowledge of a fire should FIRST notify the

   A. Station Department Office
   B. Fire Department
   C. Desk Trainmaster
   D. Station Supervisor

2. If bulletin order number 1 was issued on January 2, bulletins are being issued at the monthly average of

   A. 8   B. 10   C. 12   D. 14

3. It is clear from the bulletin that

   A. employees are expected to be expert fire fighters
   B. many fires occur on the transit system
   C. train service is usually suspended whenever a fire occurs
   D. some fires are extinguished without the help of the Fire Department

4. From the information furnished in this bulletin, it can be assumed that the

   A. Station Department office handles a considerable number of telephone calls
   B. Superintendent Investigates the handling of all subway fires
   C. Fire Department is notified only in ease of large fires
   D. employee first having knowledge of the fire must call all 4 extensions

5. The PROBABLE reason for notifying the Fire Department even when the fire has been extinguished by a subway employee is because the Fire Department is

   A. a city agency
   B. still responsible to check the fire
   C. concerned with fire prevention
   D. required to clean up after the fire

6. Information about the fire NOT specifically required is

   A. track   B. time of day   C. station   D. division

Questions 7-10.

DIRECTIONS: Questions 7 through 10 are to be answered on the basis of the paragraph on fire fighting shown below. When answering these questions, refer to this paragraph.

FIRE FIGHTING

A security officer should remember the cardinal rule that water or soda acid fire extinguishers should not be used on any electrical fire, and apply it in the case of a fire near the third rail. In addition, security officers should familiarize themselves with all available fire alarms and fire-fighting equipment within their assigned posts. Use of the fire alarm should bring responding Fire Department apparatus quickly to the scene. Familiarity with the fire-fighting equipment near his post would help in putting out incipient fires. Any man calling for the Fire Department should remain outside so that he can direct the Fire Department to the fire. As soon as possible thereafter, the special inspection desk must be notified, and a complete written report of the fire, no matter how small, must be submitted to this office. The security officer must give the exact time and place it started, who discovered it, how it was extinguished, the damage done, cause of same, list of any injured persons with the extent of their injuries, and the name of the Fire Chief in charge. All defects noticed by the security officer concerning the fire alarm or any fire-fighting equipment must be reported to the special inspection department.

7. It would be PROPER to use water to put out a fire in a(n)

   A. electric motor   B. electric switch box
   C. waste paper trash can   D. electric generator

8. After calling the Fire Department from a street box to report a fire, the security officer should then

   A. return to the fire and help put it out
   B. stay outside and direct the Fire Department to the fire
   C. find a phone and call his boss
   D. write out a report for the special inspection desk

9. A security officer is required to submit a complete written report of a fire

   A. two weeks after the fire
   B. the day following the fire
   C. as soon as possible
   D. at his convenience

10. In his report of a fire, it is NOT necessary for the security officer to state

    A. time and place of the fire
    B. who discovered the fire
    C. the names of persons injured
    D. quantity of Fire Department equipment used

Questions 11-16.

DIRECTIONS: Questions 11 through 16 are to be answered on the basis of the Notice given below. Refer to this Notice in answering these questions.

NOTICE

Your attention is called to Route Request Buttons that are installed on all new type Interlocking Home Signals where there is a choice of route in the midtown area. The route request button is to be operated by the motorman when the home signal is at danger and no call-on is displayed or when improper route is displayed.

To operate, the motorman will press the button for the desiredroute as indicated under each button; a light will then go on over the buttons to inform the motorman that his request has been registered in the tower.

If the towerman desires to give the motorman a route other than the one he selected, the towerman will cancel out the light over the route selection buttons. The motorman will then accept the route given.

If no route or call-on is given, the motorman will sound his whistle for the signal maintainer, secure his train, and call the desk trainmaster.

11. The official titles of the two classes of employee whose actions would MOST frequently be affected by the contents of this notice are

    A. motorman and trainmaster
    B. signal maintainer and trainmaster
    C. towerman and motorman
    D. signal maintainer and towerman

12. A motorman should use a route request button when

    A. the signal indicates proceed on main line
    B. a call-on is displayed
    C. the signal indicates stop
    D. the signal indicates proceed on diverging route

13. The PROPER way to request a route is to 13._____

    A. press the button corresponding to the desired route
    B. press the button a number of times to correspond with the number of the route requested
    C. stop at the signal and blow four short blasts
    D. stop at the signal and telephone the tower

14. The motorman will know that his requested route has been registered in the tower if 14._____

    A. a light comes on over the route request buttons
    B. an acknowledging signal is sounded on the tower horn
    C. the light in the route request button goes dark
    D. the home signal continues to indicate stop

15. Under certain conditions, when stopped at such home signal, the motorman must signal 15._____
    for a signal maintainer and call the desk trainmaster.
    Such condition exists when, after standing awhile,

    A. the towerman continues to give the wrong route
    B. the towerman does not acknowledge the signal
    C. no route or call-on is given
    D. the light over the route request buttons is cancelled out

16. It is clear that route request buttons 16._____

    A. eliminate train delays due to signals at junctions
    B. keep the towerman alert
    C. force motormen and towermen to be more careful
    D. are a more accurate form of communication than the whistle.

Questions 17-22.

DIRECTIONS: Questions 17 through 22 are to be answered on the basis of the instructions for removal of paper given below. Read these instructions carefully before answering these questions.

GENERAL INSTRUCTIONS FOR REMOVAL OF PAPER

When a cleaner's work schedule calls for the bagging of paper, he will remove paper from the waste paper receptacles, bag it, and place the bags at the head end of the platform, where they will be picked up by the work train. He will fill bags with paper to a weight that can be carried without danger of personal injury, as porters are forbidden to drag bags of paper over the platform. Cleaners are responsible that all bags of paper are arranged so as to prevent their falling from the platform to tracks, and so as to not interfere with passenger traffic.

17. A GOOD reason for removing the paper from receptacles and placing it in bags is that 17._____
    bags are more easily

    A. stored   B. weighed   C. handled   D. emptied

18. The *head end* of a local station platform is the end 18.____

    A. in the direction that trains are running
    B. nearest to which the trains stop
    C. where there is an underpass to the other side
    D. at which the change booth is located

19. The MOST likely reason for having the filled bags placed at the head end of the station 19.____
    rather than at the other end is that

    A. a special storage space is provided there for them
    B. this end of the platform is farthest from the passengers
    C. most porters' closets are located near the head end
    D. the work train stops at this end to pick them up

20. Limiting the weight to which the bags can be filled is PROBABLY done to 20.____

    A. avoid having too many ripped or broken bags
    B. protect the porter against possible rupture
    C. make sure that all bags are filled fairly evenly
    D. insure that, when stored, the bags will not fall to the track

21. The MOST important reason for not allowing filled bags to be dragged over the platform 21.____
    is that the bags

    A. could otherwise be loaded too heavily
    B. might leave streaks on the platform
    C. would wear out too quickly
    D. might spill paper on the platform

22. The instructions do NOT hold a porter responsible for a bag of paper which 22.____

    A. is torn due to dragging over a platform
    B. falls on a passenger because it was poorly stacked
    C. falls to the track without being pushed
    D. is ripped open by school children

Questions 23-25.

DIRECTIONS: Questions 23 through 25 are to be answered on the basis of the situation described below. Consider the facts given in this situation when answering these questions.

SITUATION

A new detergent that is to be added to water and the resulting mixture just wiped on any surface has been tested by the station department and appeared to be excellent. However, you notice, after inspecting a large number of stations that your porters have cleaned with this detergent, that the surfaces cleaned are not as clean as they formerly were when the old method was used.

23. The MAIN reason for the station department testing the new detergent in the first place was to make certain that

    A. it was very simple to use
    B. a little bit would go a long way
    C. there was no stronger detergent on the market
    D. it was superior to anything formerly used

24. The MAIN reason that such a poor cleaning job resulted was MOST likely due to the

    A. porters being lax on the job
    B. detergent not being as good as expected
    C. incorrect amount of water being mixed with the detergent
    D. fact that the surfaces cleaned needed to be scrubbed

25. The reason for inspecting a number of stations was to

    A. determine whether all porters did the same job
    B. insure that the result of the cleaning job was the same in each location
    C. be certain that the detergent was used in each station inspected
    D. see whether certain surfaces cleaned better than others

KEY (CORRECT ANSWERS)

1.	A	11.	C
2.	C	12.	C
3.	D	13.	A
4.	A	14.	A
5.	C	15.	C
6.	B	16.	D
7.	C	17.	C
8.	B	18.	A
9.	C	19.	D
10.	D	20.	B

21. C
22. D
23. D
24. B
25. B

ARITHMETIC

EXAMINATION SECTION
TEST 1

DIRECTIONS: Each question or incomplete statement is followed by several suggested answers or completions. Select the one that BEST answers the question or completes the statement. *PRINT THE LETTER OF THE CORRECT ANSWER IN THE SPACE AT THE RIGHT.*

1. From 30983 subtract 29998. The answer should be
   A. 985   B. 995   C. 1005   D. 1015   1.____

2. From $2537.75 subtract $1764.28. The answer should be
   A. $763.58   B. $773.47   C. $774.48   D. $873.58   2.____

3. From 254211 subtract 76348. The answer should be
   A. 177863   B. 177963   C. 187963   D. 188973   3.____

4. Divide 4025 by 35. The answer should be
   A. 105   B. 109   C. 115   D. 125   4.____

5. Multiply 0.35 by 2764. The answer should be
   A. 997.50   B. 967.40   C. 957.40   D. 834.40   5.____

6. Multiply 1367 by 0.50. The answer should be
   A. 6.8350   B. 68.350   C. 683.50   D. 6835.0   6.____

7. Multiply 841 by 0.01. The answer should be
   A. 0.841   B. 8.41   C. 84.1   D. 841   7.____

8. Multiply 1962 by 25. The answer should be
   A. 47740   B. 48460   C. 48950   D. 49050   8.____

9. Multiply 905 by 0.05. The answer should be
   A. 452.5   B. 45.25   C. 4.525   D. 0.4525   9.____

10. Multiply 8.93 by 4.7. The answer should be
   A. 41.971   B. 40.871   C. 4.1971   D. 4.0871   10.____

11. Multiply 25 by 763. The answer should be
   A. 18075   B. 18875   C. 19075   D. 20965   11.____

12. Multiply 2530 by 0.10. The answer should be
   A. 2.5300   B. 25.300   C. 253.00   D. 2530.0   12.____

13. Multiply 3053 by 0.25. The answer should be   13._____

    A. 76.325   B. 86.315   C. 763.25   D. 863.15

14. Multiply 6204 by 0.35. The answer should be   14._____

    A. 2282.40   B. 2171.40   C. 228.24   D. 217.14

15. Multiply $.35 by 7619. The answer should be   15._____

    A. $2324.75   B. $2565.65   C. $2666.65   D. $2756.75

16. Multiply 6513 by 45. The answer should be   16._____

    A. 293185   B. 293085   C. 292185   D. 270975

17. Multiply 3579 by 70. The answer should be   17._____

    A. 25053.0   B. 240530   C. 250530   D. 259530

18. A class had an average of 24 words correct on a spelling test. The class average on this   18._____
    spelling test was 80%.
    The AVERAGE number of words missed on this test was

    A. 2   B. 4   C. 6   D. 8

19. In which one of the following is 24 renamed as a product of primes?   19._____

    A. 2 x 6 x 2   B. 8 x 3 x 1
    C. 2 x 2 x 3 x 2   D. 3 x 4 x 2

Questions 20-23.

DIRECTIONS: In answering Questions 20 through 23, perform the indicated operation. Select the BEST answer from the choices below.

20. Add: 7068   20._____
         2807
         9434
         6179

    A. 26,488   B. 24,588   C. 25,488   D. 25,478

21. Divide: 75√45555   21._____

    A. 674   B. 607.4   C. 6074   D. 60.74

22. Multiply: 907   22._____
              x806

    A. 73,142   B. 13,202   C. 721,042   D. 731,042

23. Subtract: 60085   23._____
              -47194

    A. 12,891   B. 13,891   C. 12,991   D. 12,871

24. A librarian reported that 1/5% of all books taken out last school year had not been returned.
    If 85,000 books were borrowed from the library, how many were not returned?

    A. 170   B. 425   C. 1,700   D. 4,250

25. At 40 miles per hour, how many minutes would it take to travel 12 miles?

    A. 30   B. 18   C. 15   D. 20

KEY (CORRECT ANSWERS)

1. A
2. B
3. A
4. C
5. B

6. C
7. B
8. D
9. B
10. A

11. C
12. C
13. C
14. B
15. C

16. B
17. C
18. C
19. C
20. C

21. B
22. D
23. A
24. A
25. B

SOLUTIONS TO PROBLEMS

1. 30,983 - 29,998 = 985

2. $2537.75 - $1764.28 = $773.47

3. 254,211 - 76,348 = 177,863

4. 4025 ÷ 35 = 115

5. (.35)(2764) = 967.4

6. (1367)(.50) = 683.5

7. (841)(.01) = 8.41

8. (1962)(25) = 49,050

9. (905)(.05) = 45.25

10. (8.93)(4.7) = 41.971

11. (25)(763) = 19,075

12. (2530)(.10) = 253

13. (3053)(.25) = 763.25

14. (6204)(.35) = 2171.4

15. ($.35)(7619) = $2666.65

16. (6513)(45) = 293,085

17. (3579)(70) = 250,530

18. 24 ÷ .80 = 30. Then, 30 - 24 = 6 words

19. 24 = 2 x 2 x 3 x 2, where each number is a prime.

20. 7068 ÷ 2807 + 9434 + 6179 = 25,488

21. 45,555 ÷ 75 = 607.4

22. (907)(806) = 731,042

23. 60,085 - 47,194 = 12,891

24. (1/5%)(85,000) = (.002)(85,000) = 170 books

25. Let x = number of minutes. Then, $\dfrac{40}{60} = \dfrac{12}{x}$. Solving, x = 18

TEST 2

DIRECTIONS: Each question or incomplete statement is followed by several **suggested** answers or completions. Select the one that BEST answers the question or completes the statement. *PRINT THE LETTER OF THE CORRECT ANSWER IN THE SPACE AT THE RIGHT.*

1. The sum of 57901 + 34762 is   1.____
   A. 81663   B. 82663   C. 91663   D. 92663

2. The sum of 559 + 448 + 362 + 662 is   2.____
   A. 2121   B. 2031   C. 2021   D. 1931

3. The sum of 36153 + 28624 + 81379 is   3.____
   A. 136156   B. 146046   C. 146146   D. 146156

4. The sum of 742 + 9197 + 8972 is   4.____
   A. 19901   B. 18911   C. 18801   D. 17921

5. The sum of 7989 + 8759 + 2726 is   5.____
   A. 18455   B. 18475   C. 19464   D. 19474

6. The sum of $111.55 + $95.05 + $38.80 is   6.____
   A. $234.40   B. $235.30   C. $245.40   D. $254.50

7. The sum of 1302 + 46187 + 92610 + 4522 is   7.____
   A. 144621   B. 143511   C. 134621   D. 134521

8. The sum of 47953 + 58041 + 63022 + 22333 is   8.____
   A. 170248   B. 181349   C. 191349   D. 200359

9. The sum of 76563 + 43693 + 38521 + 50987 + 72723 is   9.____
   A. 271378   B. 282386   C. 282487   D. 292597

10. The sum of 85923 + 97211 + 11333 + 4412 + 22533 is   10.____
    A. 209302   B. 212422   C. 221412   D. 221533

11. The sum of 4299 + 54163 + 89765 + 1012 + 38962 is   11.____
    A. 188201   B. 188300   C. 188301   D. 189311

12. The sum of 48526 + 709 + 11534 + 80432 + 6096 is   12.____
    A. 135177   B. 139297   C. 147297   D. 149197

13. The sum of $407.62 + $109.01 + $68.44 + $378.68 is   13.____
    A. $963.75   B. $964.85   C. $973.65   D. $974.85

14. From 40614 subtract 4697. The answer should be

    A. 35917 B. 35927 C. 36023 D. 36027

15. From 81773 subtract 5717. The answer should be

    A. 75964 B. 76056 C. 76066 D. 76956

16. From $1755.35 subtract $1201.75. The answer should be

    A. $542.50 B. $544.50 C. $553.60 D. $554.60

17. From $2402.10 subtract $998.85. The answer should be

    A. $1514.35 B. $1504.25 C. $1413.25 D. $1403.25

18. Add: 12 1/2
            2 1/2
            3 1/2

    A. 17 B. 17 1/4 C. 17 3/4 D. 18

19. Subtract: 150
                -80

    A. 70 B. 80 C. 130 D. 150

20. After cleaning up some lots in the city dump, five cleanup crews loaded the following amounts of garbage on trucks:
    Crew No. 1 loaded 2 1/4 tons
    Crew No. 2 loaded 3 tons
    Crew No. 3 loaded 1 1/4 tons
    Crew No. 4 loaded 2 1/4 tons
    Crew No. 5 loaded 1/2 ton.
    The TOTAL number of tons of garbage loaded was

    A. 8 1/4 B. 8 3/4 C. 9 D. 9 1/4

21. Subtract: 17 3/4
                 -7 1/4

    A. 7 1/2 B. 10 1/2 C. 14 1/4 D. 17 3/4

22. Yesterday, Tom and Bill each received 10 leaflets about rat control. They were supposed to distribute one leaflet to each supermarket in the neighborhood. When the day was over, Tom had 8 leaflets left. Bill had no leaflets left.
    How many supermarkets got leaflets yesterday?

    A. 8 B. 10 C. 12 D. 18

23. What is 2/3 of 1 1/8?

    A. 1 11/16 B. 3/4 C. 3/8 D. 4 1/3

24. A farmer bought a load of 120 bushels of corn.
    After he fed 45 bushels to his hogs, what fraction of his supply remained?

    A. 5/8 B. 3/5 C. 3/8 D. 4/7

25. In the numeral 3,159,217, the 2 is in the _____ column. 25._____

    A. hundreds   B. units   C. thousands   D. tens

KEY (CORRECT ANSWERS)

1.	D	11.	A
2.	B	12.	C
3.	D	13.	A
4.	B	14.	A
5.	D	15.	B
6.	C	16.	C
7.	A	17.	D
8.	C	18.	D
9.	C	19.	A
10.	C	20.	D

21. B
22. C
23. B
24. A
25. A

SOLUTIONS TO PROBLEMS

1. 57,901 + 34,762 = 92,663

2. 559 + 448 + 362 + 662 = 2031

3. 36,153 + 28,624 + 81,379 = 146,156

4. 742 + 9197 + 8972 = 18,911

5. 7989 + 8759 + 2726 = 19,474

6. $111.55 + $95.05 + $38.80 = $245.40

7. 1302 + 46,187 + 92,610 + 4522 = 144,621

8. 47,953 + 58,041 + 63,022 + 22,333 = 191,349

9. 76,563 + 45,693 + 38,521 + 50,987 + 72,723 = 282,487

10. 85,923 + 97,211 + 11,333 + 4412 + 22,533 = 221,412

11. 4299 + 54,163 + 89,765 + 1012 + 38,962 = 188,201

12. 48,526 + 709 + 11,534 + 80,432 + 6096 = 147,297

13. $407.62 + $109.01 + $68.44 + $378.68 = $963.75

14. 40,614 - 4697 = 35,917

15. 81,773 - 5717 = 76,056

16. $1755.35 - $1201.75 = $553.60

17. $2402.10 - $998.85 = $1403.25

18. 12 1/2 + 2 1/4 + 3 1/4 = 17 4/4 = 18

19. 150 - 80 = 70

20. 2 1/4 + 3 + 1 1/4 + 2 1/4 + 1/2 = 8 5/4 = 9 1/4 tons

21. 17 3/4 - 7 1/4 = 10 2/4 = 10 1/2

22. 10 + 10 - 8 - 0 = 12 supermarkets

23. $(\frac{2}{3})(1\frac{1}{8}) = (\frac{2}{3})(\frac{9}{8}) = \frac{18}{24} = \frac{3}{4}$

24. 120 - 45 = 75. Then, $\frac{75}{120} = \frac{5}{8}$

25. The number 2 is in the hundreds column of 3,159,217

TEST 3

DIRECTIONS: Each question or incomplete statement is followed by several suggested answers or completions. Select the one that BEST answers the question or completes the statement. *PRINT THE LETTER OF THE CORRECT ANSWER IN THE SPACE AT THE RIGHT.*

1. The distance covered in three minutes by a subway train traveling at 30 mph is _____ mile(s).   1._____

   A. 3   B. 2   C. 1 1/2   D. 1

2. A crate contains 3 pieces of equipment weighing 73, 84, and 47 pounds, respectively. The empty crate weighs 16 pounds.   2._____
   If the crate is lifted by 4 trackmen, each trackman lifting one corner of the crate, the AVERAGE number of pounds lifted by each of the trackmen is

   A. 68   B. 61   C. 55   D. 51

3. The weight per foot of a length of square-bar 4" x 4" in cross-section, as compared with one 2" x 2" in cross-section, is _____ as much.   3._____

   A. twice   B. 2 1/2 times
   C. 3 times   D. 4 times

4. An order for 360 feet of 2" x 8" lumber is shipped in 20-foot lengths.   4._____
   The MAXIMUM number of 9-foot pieces that can be cut from this shipment is

   A. 54   B. 40   C. 36   D. 18

5. If a trackman gets $10.40 per hour and time and one-half for working over 40 hours, his gross salary for a week in which he worked 44 hours should be   5._____

   A. $457.60   B. $478.40   C. $499.20   D. $514.80

6. If a section of ballast 6'-0" wide, 8'-0" long, and 2'-6" deep is excavated, the amount of ballast removed is _____ cu. feet.   6._____

   A. 96   B. 104   C. 120   D. 144

7. The sum of 7'2 3/4", 0'-2 7/8", 3'-0", 4'-6 3/8", and 1'-9 1/4" is   7._____

   A. 16'-8 1/4"   B. 16'-8 3/4"   C. 16'-9 1/4"   D. 16'-9 3/4"

8. The sum of 3 1/16", 4 1/4", 2 5/8", and 5 7/16" is   8._____

   A. 15 3/16"   B. 15 1/4"   C. 15 3/8"   D. 15 1/2"

9. Add: $51.79, $29.39, and $8.98.   9._____
   The CORRECT answer is

   A. $78.97   B. $88.96   C. $89.06   D. $90.16

10. Add: $72.07 and $31.54. Then subtract $25.75.   10._____
    The CORRECT answer is

    A. $77.86   B. $82.14   C. $88.96   D. $129.36

11. Start with $82.47. Then subtract $25.50, $4.75, and 35¢.
    The CORRECT answer is
    A. $30.60　　B. $51.87　　C. $52.22　　D. $65.25　　11.____

12. Add: $19.35 and $37.75. Then subtract $9.90 and $19.80.
    The CORRECT answer is
    A. $27.40　　B. $37.00　　C. $37.30　　D. $47.20　　12.____

13. Add:　$153
    　　　　114
    　　　　210
    　　　+186
    A. $657　　B. $663　　C. $713　　D. $757　　13.____

14. Add:　$64.91
    　　　　13.53
    　　　　19.27
    　　　　20.00
    　　　+72.84
    A. $170.25　　B. $178.35　　C. $180.45　　D. $190.55　　14.____

15. Add:　1963
    　　　　1742
    　　　+2497
    A. 6202　　B. 6022　　C. 5212　　D. 5102　　15.____

16. Add:　206
    　　　　709
    　　　　1342
    　　　+2076
    A. 3432　　B. 3443　　C. 4312　　D. 4333　　16.____

17. Subtract:　$190.76
    　　　　　 -　.99
    A. $189.97　　B. $189.87　　C. $189.77　　D. $189.67　　17.____

18. From 99876 subtract 85397. The answer should be
    A. 14589　　B. 14521　　C. 14479　　D. 13589　　18.____

19. From $876.51 subtract $92.89. The answer should be
    A. $773.52　　B. $774.72　　C. $783.62　　D. $784.72　　19.____

20. From 70935 subtract 49489. The answer should be
    A. 20436　　B. 21446　　C. 21536　　D. 21546　　20.____

21. From $391.55 subtract $273.45. The answer should be 21.____
    A. $118.10   B. $128.20   C. $178.10   D. $218.20

22. When 119 is subtracted from the sum of 2016 + 1634, the answer is 22.____
    A. 2460   B. 3531   C. 3650   D. 3769

23. Multiply 35 x 65 x 15. The answer should be 23.____
    A. 2275   B. 24265   C. 31145   D. 34125

24. Multiply: 4.06 24.____
              x.031
    A. 1.2586   B. .12586   C. .02586   D. .1786

25. When 65 is added to the result of 14 multiplied by 13, the answer is 25.____
    A. 92   B. 182   C. 247   D. 16055

KEY (CORRECT ANSWERS)

1.	C	11.	B
2.	C	12.	A
3.	D	13.	B
4.	C	14.	D
5.	B	15.	A
6.	C	16.	D
7.	C	17.	C
8.	C	18.	C
9.	D	19.	C
10.	A	20.	B

21. A
22. B
23. D
24. B
25. C

SOLUTIONS TO PROBLEMS

1. Let x = distance. Then, $\frac{30}{60} = \frac{x}{3}$ Solving, x = 1 1/2 miles

2. (73 + 84 + 47 + 16) ÷ 4 = 55 pounds

3. (4 x 4) ÷ (2 x 2) = a ratio of 4 to 1.

4. 20 ÷ 9 = 2 2/9, rounded down to 2 pieces. Then, (360 ÷ 20)(2) = 36

5. Salary = ($10.40)(40) + ($15.60)(4) = $478.40

6. (6)(8)(2 1/2) = 120 cu.ft.

7. $7'2\frac{3}{4}" + 0'2\frac{7}{8}" + 3'0" + 4'6\frac{3}{8}" + 1'9\frac{1}{4}" = 15'19\frac{18}{8}" = 15'21\frac{1}{4}" = 16'9\frac{1}{4}"$

8. $3\frac{1}{16}" + 4\frac{1}{4}" + 2\frac{5}{8}" + 5\frac{7}{16}" = 14\frac{22}{16}" = 15\frac{3}{8}"$

9. $51.79 + $29.39 + $8.98 = $90.16

10. $72.07 + $31.54 = $103.61. Then, $103.61 - $25.75 = $77.86

11. $82.47 - $25.50 - $4.75 - $0.35 = $51.87

12. $19.35 + $37.75 = $57.10. Then, $57.10 - $9.90 - $19.80 = $27.40

13. $153 + $114 + $210 + $186 = $663

14. $64.91 + $13.53 + $19.27 + $20.00 + $72.84 = $190.55

15. 1963 + 1742 + 2497 = 6202

16. 206 + 709 + 1342 + 2076 = 4333

17. $190.76 - .99 = $189.77

18. 99,876 - 85,397 = 14,479

19. $876.51 - $92.89 = $783.62

20. 70,935 - 49,489 = 21,446

21. $391.55 - $273.45 = $118.10

22. (2016 + 1634) - 119 = 3650 - 119 = 3531

23. (35)(65)(15) = 34,125

24. (4.06)(.031) = .12586

25. 65 + (14)(13) = 65 + 182 = 247

www.ingramcontent.com/pod-product-compliance
Lightning Source LLC
Chambersburg PA
CBHW082148300426
44117CB00016B/2658